# BROKEN CHAINS

## PRINCIPLES TO OVERCOMING ADDICTION

Randy Nurmi

WestBow
PRESS
A DIVISION OF THOMAS NELSON

WestBow Press books may be ordered through booksellers or by contacting:

WestBow Press
A Division of Thomas Nelson
1663 Liberty Drive
Bloomington, IN 47403
www.westbowpress.com
1-(866) 928-1240

Additional copies are available from:
Pure Word Ministries
Boise ID

Phone: (208) 322-3073
Email: cjohnson@pureword.org

To order more workbooks, please contact us. Proceeds from these sales allow us to continue the publication of this material.  Our cost has been kept at a minimum to allow those in need to still have access to this workbook.

If our materials are helpful and the Lord moves your heart to support this ministry, we would pray you would be obedient to do whatever He instructs you to do.

ISBN: 978-1-4497-0513-8 (sc)
ISBN: 978-1-4497-0586-2 (e)

Library of Congress Control Number: 2010935767

Printed in the United States of America

WestBow Press rev. date: 1/10/2011

# Table of Contents

# Author's Acknowledgements

## Pastor Randy would like to thank:

**Jesus** my LORD and Savior to whom all thanksgiving, glory, and honor is owed. He saved me eternally, spiritual, mentally, and physically. He gave me life and restored my mind so I could write this to help others who are still in the valley of decision.

**Tamie** my wife and TRUE soul mate, who has loved me through thick, thin, and tough times and still puts up with all my spiritual development and psychological scares and prolonged weirdness.

My children **Zachary, Tiffany, Josiah, Isaiah, and Cameron** who have been my best teachers in life. Thanks for loving me in a way my heart will never understand, but will always cherish and treasure.

**Chris Johnson** my faithful assistant, without the honesty and boldness to speak the truth to me this would have not have the present form and flow. Thanks for all the patience, editing, and hours you dedicated to this project.

**Bob Caldwell,** my only Pastor, thanks for investing in me by illustrating and leading me to a higher standard and teaching me to never settle for the good or what would be accepted by others as okay, but to always aspire for the very best in Christ, because the rewards in the suffering bless the most and bless many. **Cathy Caldwell,** his wife, whose smile has brought countless hope and shows mercy to many. Thank you both for your love. Your Spirit-filled lives inspire many.

**Doug McFerrin,** the man who can communicate the Gospel through artwork and the artwork words cannot express, but the eyes of the heart understand.

**Linda Smith,** without her expertise and faithfulness in patience, no one would be able to read this or have the opportunity to grow in hope, faith, and love this manuscript will provide.

**Jessica Toussau,** thanks for faithful assistance for the graphic design.

**Mary Anne Tschannen**, thanks for your discerning eye during the editing process.

**Rick Anderson** and **John Elliott** of "All American Publishing," thank you for having enough belief in the LORD in me, this project, your financial contributions, and recognizing the hand of the LORD upon it.

Many thanks need to be acknowledged and given to all who have been served through the **Pure Word Ministry**, participated in, and have been restored by the Lord's grace and mercy through the years. Thank you for hearing, seeing, believing, and living out the truth that is written in the Bible for anyone who will open his or her hearts to this fantastic gift called sobriety.

All those who were brave enough to submit their testimonies for this project and allow our Savior to use them as instruments of hope and vessels of courage.

All those who abused me. Now some may think this a strange thank you, but Jesus allowed the use of all of them in my life to show the contrast of the dark threads they knit in the fabric of my early life. Those dark threads are what made the blue threads woven by Jesus so bright. I have used that contrast to make His life and love to shine brighter.

## Resource Acknowledgements and Permissions:

The Preacher's Outline & Sermon Bible, Gal-Col; published by Leadership Ministries Worldwide; © Alpha-Omega Ministries, Inc. 1996; Used by permission; All rights reserved throughout the world.

(OLB)  On-linebible.net. Used by permission.

The portion 'Love Is' is copied from pages 217 to 219 in the Self-Confrontation manual, which is written and published by the Biblical Counseling Foundation (BCF). Although BCF has granted permission to copy this portion from their materials, this does not imply that the Biblical Counseling Foundation is in agreement with the other portions of this work, nor is BCF in any other way associated with this organization. The Biblical Counseling Foundation does not receive monetary gain from the sale of this workbook.

# About Pure Word Ministries

Pure Word Ministries began in February 1987 out of an answer to prayer and a desire to have a meeting focused on Jesus Christ and to acknowledge His ability to set individuals free from bondage to sin and fear. God's Word, the Bible, tells us it is sufficient for all areas of life and it will equip us thoroughly for all areas of ministry (2 Timothy 3:16-17).

Because of this, we now offer assistance for not only alcohol and drug issues, but also for other addictive behaviors. Jesus came to set people free, and the focus of this ministry is to see the people set free from the issues that hold them in bondage to sin. Our teaching model offers an effective approach in keeping focus on the issues at hand and the supremacy of Jesus Christ in our lives.

Some have misconstrued our vision, methods, and intent because of our Christ-centered format, but with these principles, we live out the reality that it is God's grace and mercy that has truly restored our lives. We have found great success in keeping this consistent format. Though some may fall back into sinful behaviors, when they return, they see the love of Christ displayed in the format and people in the same consistent manner.

As a result of my desire and experience, this workbook was developed through years of counseling individuals. The principles in these lessons help build sensitivity to our need for sobriety in all areas of life, not just in the specific areas of our struggles. They are called principles because they are something we must put into practice as Christians during our walk in Christ.

Steps, on the other hand, are often thought of as something that can be attempted, worked on, completed, and forgotten. They often develop pride within us because we naturally think we have conquered or completed them on our own.

In truth, there is only one step we can take that will save us from the addictions, fear, bondage, and sin that we suffer from. We don't want to project a false idea or security that misrepresents the message of the Gospel. The only way to receive the saving knowledge of Jesus Christ is to come to our senses, recognize we are sinners in need of a Savior, and humble ourselves before a most Holy God. After this we are enabled to repent of our sins, ask Him to forgive us, and to come into our hearts by faith. All of this occurs because of God's wonderful grace. ***Ephesians 2:8-9***, *"For by grace you have been saved through faith, and that not of yourselves; it is the gift of God, not of works, lest anyone should boast."* ***Titus 3:4-7***, *"But when the kindness and the love of God our Savior toward man appeared, not by works of righteousness which we have done, but according to His mercy He saved us, through the washing of regeneration and renewing of the Holy Spirit, whom He poured out on us abundantly through Jesus Christ our Savior, that having been justified by His grace we should become heirs according to the hope of eternal life."*

Paul told us to work out our salvation with fear and trembling and these principles represent this as an ongoing process of sanctification that is birthed within our hearts and manifested through our actions. We are enabled to continue this process through the power of His Spirit, mercy, and love. It is ushered in through grace and we are kept through the power of His Word.

We pray these principles will be a small help to you in your walk and endeavor as you persevere to please the One who has saved you and gives you the awesome gift of sobriety day by day. If allowed to do their work, these principles will begin to work on our denial and begin to allow the process of humbling and breaking to take place within us. The work of the Holy Spirit is to convict us of our sin and draw us to Christ.

# Jesus Came to Heal the Broken Hearted

Randy Nurmi was six years old when his adoptive father was beaten in a barroom brawl and later died. On the evening his dad died he told Randy he was the man of the house and he could never cry again. He believed that lie for almost twenty years. His dad's death was just one brief scenario in a childhood decimated by almost every form of abuse imaginable.

Born in Okinawa, he was just six months old when an angry adult ripped his arm from his body. A few months later, with the arm reattached, he was shipped off to America, adopted by an alcoholic father and an enabling mother. "My father started giving me alcohol when I was a baby. He'd take me down to the bars; give me Orange Crush pop and shots of vodka. Then he and his drinking buddies would line up their shot glasses and walk me down the bar. Whoever's shot glass I knocked over would have to buy the next round. My dad died when he was just 42." By then Randy was already a fighter.

At 6½, he was smoking cigarettes and running around with rowdy teenagers. His mom didn't like alcohol and was upset when she smelled it on his breath, but she was totally ignorant of marijuana. By the time Randy was seven he was getting stoned regularly. At eight, he was dealing drugs.

About the same time his widowed mother took him to a Lutheran conference. "I remember all these people studying scriptures and praying for me. It was the strangest thing, the Holy Spirit spoke to me and said 'give me all your pain,' but then I remembered I wasn't suppose to cry, my father had told me I could never cry again. I got up, ran out of the room, and the devil told me I'd blasphemed the Lord by leaving the room. I didn't understand why the Lord would tell me to do something I couldn't do."

For as long as he could remember, Randy owned, not one or two, but many different Bible translations. Early on he acquired an incredible gift for Scripture memorization. "I've always had the ability to look at a verse, memorize it, and go on. I was doing that from the time I was a little kid but there was no context. I was a very angry child." Yet at night, alone in his bed, the little boy who could not cry would crawl under his covers and preach to an imaginary crowd. "Weird, huh?" he chuckles. The fascination with God's Word distracted him from a day-to-day existence that was far from heavenly.

His mother worked in the woolen mills in Pendleton, Oregon. For a while she left Randy unsupervised. He became more difficult and unruly. She hired babysitters, first a girl, then a man. They both assaulted him sexually. His mother's remarriage only made things worse. "I couldn't understand why everybody wanted to do that to me," Randy said. "I kept thinking I was asking for it, even though I hated it."

When his mother married his present step dad, Randy was a very angry and bitter boy. "I made their lives totally miserable." As a rebellious stepchild, he tried to split up the marriage. During the same period, Randy's drug addiction grew to daily use of marijuana and whatever else he could get his hands on. "LSD, mushrooms, you name it. Anything I wanted was easy to acquire." The school was ready to incarcerate him. "Counselors recommended the military." Instead, he left home at 15, determined to be "a big gangster. I thought I was good at selling drugs and staying out of trouble." His alcoholism gained him notoriety. "I was just in a downward spiral," he said. He left Oregon at 18 and came to Boise where he survived for the next eight years selling cocaine.

"My drugs of choice were alcohol and cocaine. I drank two cases of beer and a fifth of Black Velvet whiskey every day for the last six years of my drug career. I also had a daily cocaine habit of $500 - $900. I needed that to counteract the whiskey. I did that 24 hours a day. "I blacked out all of 1983," Randy says. "No, that's not true, I remember the Super Bowl. Other than the Super Bowl, I don't remember a thing."

When he came to, he was a father. "I had a little boy named Zachary. That was the first time I ever thought I had a problem. However, my denial was so high I wouldn't accept it, and I couldn't quit. Fear and anger were my best friends. I was afraid because of the people I knew and the things I did that if I quit I'd be a threat and that was life threatening."

Surprisingly, Randy still had good knowledge of the Bible—knowledge he used to convince himself he could not be saved. "One night I was listening to really loud music and I woke up this little Baptist Sunday school teacher. He came over to witness to me about the love of Jesus. I spent the whole night quoting scripture trying to convince him I was going to Hell."

Six months later, at 2:21 in the morning on January 25, 1985, Randy was ready to take a direct trip to the hereafter. He was 26 and "ready to end my life," he says. "When I finally did meet Jesus, it was at the end of a shotgun barrel. The Lord spoke to me just as clearly as the enemy had spoken to me years before, when he told me I'd blasphemed the Holy Spirit and could never be saved. The Lord spoke to me from scripture."

Randy will never forget the verse. Isaiah 30:21: "Your ears shall hear a word behind you, saying, 'This is the way, walk in it, whenever you turn to the right hand or whenever you turn to the left.'" Randy still knew hundreds of Bible verses but the words had no context. This time the verse made sense. "I knew I wasn't supposed to be afraid, that there was a better way and that I would not turn to the left or turn to the right."

He spent 18 days in detox, then a rehab facility where he met two terrific Christians. "God opened their hearts to me. They taught me the Word. I darkened the doors of Calvary Chapel for the first time in summer of 1985. I could tell Calvary was the place to be, but I didn't think I deserved it. I knew Jesus Christ had saved my life. I knew He really wanted to do something with it and I had believed a lie."

Randy wasn't quite sure how to get out from under that lie. "I'd been selling drugs for the same people since I was eight years old. They were virtual parents to me. I was really afraid to tell them I was through." Again, the Lord provided the right message from His Word. "Proverbs 16:7," Randy recalls, 'When your ways please the Lord He'll make even your enemies at peace with you.'" There have been no repercussions from the drug dealers. Nor, has Randy suffered any of the physical plights of alcoholism or drug addiction. It's really incredible.

Equally impressive are the changes the Lord made in Randy's relationship with his son's mother and her family. "She wasn't a Christian when I got saved. My being a cocaine addict, an alcoholic, and an absentee dad was one thing; Jesus freak was something else. Here I'd gone from total darkness to total light. Her family wasn't Christian. Her dad didn't think I was going to live very long, either because of my lifestyle or because he was going to throttle me."

In July of 1987, Randy and Tamie were married. The following year they started a discipleship house for other new Christians. At first, Tamie's dad thought their newfound religion was just a phase. "He'd seen people change like I had before," Randy says. "Then we started doing the discipleship house, working through our own problems, giving all the credit to Jesus Christ.

"Now," Randy says, "My father-in-law loves me like his own son. I've had the blessing of working with Calvary in a ministerial capacity almost since I first arrived. Whenever I sought to serve Him and His people, He's blessed me and lifted me up. Never in my wildest dreams did I ever think I'd be on a church staff as an assistant pastor. Even when I was first saved, I thought I'd be sent out to the mission field. Jesus put my life back together in every area Satan tried to destroy...spiritually, financially, physically. Jesus does heal."

# Learning "To Be" Instead of Learning "To Do"

Greetings my friends in Christ,

This short study is about the all-important point of allowing the grace of God to penetrate your heart instead of having it get stuck in your mind. My heart's desire is you allow it to increase your faith in simple, applicatory ways.

There are some negative issues that face us that are caused by our fallen nature and the part our wills play in the process of learning, surrendering, and yielding to the Lord when being taught by the Holy Spirit. There are tremendous benefits of allowing God to perform His will through us and all we do, as well as perplexing issues that prevent it from occurring on an everyday basis. The constant temptation we all face is in the realm of our wills when it comes to our ability to learn. It is the temptation of learning "to do" instead of learning "to be" (Phil 2:13).

I am not arguing against the truth that "faith without works" is dead. My point is simply to present a case against the propensity of leaning upon our works and knowledge alone as a confirmation that we are succeeding in God. We must remember God has told us our mark to aim for is being poor in Spirit. The standard He is looking for is the individual who recognizes it is God alone who enables and empowers him to perform what pleases Him (Is 29:19; Matt 5:3; Mark 8:34-37; John 3:30; 1 Cor 1:26-31; 2 Cor 3:5-6; 4:7).

When **learning** things we are constantly tempted to learn them to "**do them.**" We put all we learn into practice in the realms of *intellect, knowledge, and works* so we can perform and prove what we have learned. We turn to the letter of the law, which always kills. When doing this, we automatically turn to carnality instead of to the work of the Spirit. We turn to works in order to gain confidence and security. When we rest on these results in order to gain kudos from those around us, we usually find the opposite because all men are unstable, fickle, and end up only having a form of godliness and remain powerless to manifest any lasting change at all (2 Tim 3:5). We also gain the three rewards the flesh promised to give us: frustration, fatigue, and failure. God tells us to never place confidence in the flesh (Phil 3:3).

We are tempted to turn to our intellect and knowledge of religion and our religious acts. We are tempted to think the more we learn, the more security we have regarding our relationship with Him. The more we learn about certain doctrines and the better we think we can perform them causes us to believe in the fleshly results that give us false evidence of how close we are to God because we end up judging ourselves on misleading results (Job 9:20; 15:14; Ps 19:12; 139:23; 143:2; Prov 17:3; 21:2; 1 Cor 4:4-5). It causes us to turn to pride and to place confidence in our kudos that we receive from men, not God. Learning "to do" ultimately takes us further from our goals and God (Is 5:21; 47:10; Rom 12:16; 1 Cor 13:4).

However, after becoming a child of God, we receive direction from the Holy Spirit and we begin to grow and mature in Christ. We are told God has access to the surface of our hearts and He writes instructions upon them with ink that doesn't fade (Eze 36:26-27; Eph 2:10). He writes them with the Spirit which gives us life and freedom. When we allow the Holy Spirit to teach us, He gives us peace of heart without condemnation so we can believe we can learn and apply these simple instructions to our lives. <u>The difference between learning things from a human perspective and a Godly perspective is when we learn things of the Spirit, we "can be them" instead of doing them</u>. This is what enables us to experience the fruit of the Spirit which is known as the nature of Christ within us. **We are no longer** <u>doing</u> **the fruit; we** <u>become</u> **the fruit**. We become love, joy, peace, longsuffering, kind, good, faithful, gentle, and self-controlled.

Remember we come to God because of His grace through faith. We are then "born again" and "filled with His Spirit" so we become pleasing to Him because of what our faith in His Son has caused. Jesus is the propitiation for our sin. Through faith, we are now empowered to be all that we can be in the Spirit, in the Son, and in who we are today. We are a new creation in Christ and the old has passed away. We can put off the old man and put on the new man. We now have the mind of Christ and the will to use it. We have the riches in Christ that are given to us through the relationship of adoption that we received by being grafted into the trunk of God. God, being the root, now supports us through the sap that flows through the whole tree. As a branch, all we have to do is grow and **"<u>be</u>"** as a part of the tree. Now we are told to just "believe" or "trust" in God. <u>Believe</u>: John 3:18, 36; 6:29; 7:38; 14:1, 6; Acts 16:31; 22:14-16; Rom 4:5; 9:30-33; 10:3-4, 11; 1 John 3:23, 5:1-4. <u>Trust</u>: Ps 84:12; 146; Prov 16:20; Is 26:3-4; 30:18-19; Jer 17:7; Eph 1:12; 1 Peter 1:18-21; 2:4-10

How do we do this? We accomplish this through faith, believing, and trusting God will accomplish His will, purpose, and plan in us because He promises us and will be faithful to complete it. Fulfill the instruction given by the Apostle Paul in Col 2:6, "*As you therefore have received Christ Jesus the Lord, so walk in Him,…*" We do this entirely through the enablement of the grace of God through the power of faith. Remember God will be faithful, and we can rest from all of our works (Matt 11:28-30; Phil 1:6; Col 2:10; 1 Thes 3:13; 5:23-24; 2 Thes 2:16-17; Heb 13:20-21; 1 Pet 5:10).

God bless you all, have a grace-filled day and "give'em heaven" through the message of your life!

Randy Nurmi
Pastor and friend

# Lesson One: Recognition of a Problem

The purpose of this workbook is to gain a perspective on recovery that is different from that offered in the secular realm of treatment. God's Word stresses you are made into a new creation from the moment you receive Him into your heart or return to Him with all of your heart and receive from Him forgiveness from a backslidden condition. He promises to remove all of your unrighteousness and to cleanse you of all your sins.

One major difference between the philosophies of secular treatment of chemical addiction and Christianity is that secular beliefs and models state all of these maladies are diseases and have a lifetime sentence. When you allow yourself to identify these sins in this way, you cause yourself to shift blame and keep yourself from taking responsibility for your actions. God's Word states in **Ezekiel 18:20**, *"The soul who sins shall die. The son shall not bear the guilt of the father, nor the father bear the guilt of the son. The righteousness of the righteous shall be upon himself, and the wickedness of the wicked shall be upon himself."* God's Word also states these maladies and behaviors are sin and can be wiped away by exercising faith in Jesus Christ.

This does not mean temptations will always be removed from your life completely and instantaneously. Nor does it mean you won't suffer from the consequences of what you have done or sown during the periods of time you spent practicing your various behaviors or sins. Through grace, trust, and learning to rest in Christ, you are given the strength to overcome, conquer, and obtain victory in these sometimes very difficult and lifelong struggles.

The hope and prayer is you will gain a new perspective about recovery and the process you need to begin to practice. You will start to live out the promises of God you learn while going through this workbook. Before you begin with the 12 principles and their purposes, there are several areas to discuss: denial, definitions, anniversary periods, dreams, and the six R's of recovery. You must be made aware of and sensitive to these areas so you can begin to practice recognizing the warnings and past behavior patterns that have occurred or reoccurred and have kept you from the promises God has for you. By putting into practice what you learn from this workbook, you hopefully will begin to allow God to bring about effective change in your heart and life. Hopefully, you also will begin helping those who presently surround you, as well as those who may be in a similar set of circumstances and situations in the future.

Let's begin with probably the most difficult and stealth-like area to confront or understand—denial. Denial is caused by the intrinsic nature of the fallen heart. It is the self-deceived need for defense. It manifests in the refusal to admit obvious circumstances or situations have occurred in the breakdown of a healthy life.

Flesh, when used in the scriptures, usually means the sinful or carnal nature of man. Scripture declares the condition of the heart of man in its unregenerate state in, **Jeremiah 17:9**, *"The heart is deceitful above all things, and desperately wicked; who can know it?"* If this is the natural condition of your heart before Christ enters your life and heart, it is no wonder you are unable to make a righteous and balanced decision that promotes abundance in all areas of life. It also points out a greater truth. All mankind has turned away from God, and you really don't look for Him as many of you proclaim. (Ephesians 4:17-19, Romans 1:18; 2:11-16; 3:10-28)

As you look at the Areas of Life chart (see **Areas of Life**, Appendix 3), consider how many of these areas can truly be focused on or be completely devoted to at one time? Is it humanly possible to stay focused on all of them at once? The answer to this question is only one or two areas at the most. Only Jesus can focus on all of life's issues and concerns at one time. Only He can manage, control, and repair them in a balanced fashion so you gain abundant life that overflows with love, joy, peace, and fulfillment. The main areas of life are categorized into social, health, financial, legal, and spiritual. Denial can begin to affect any one of these life areas individually, but if allowed to grow and mature, it will eventually affect all of them. If allowed to progress unabated, addiction will deteriorate choices and free will.

Denial is observed in several examples in the scriptures. See the example of Aaron in the book of Exodus 32 (especially verse 24). Also see the example of King Saul to Samuel in the book of 1 Samuel 15 (especially verse 14).

**Psalms 32:3-4** *When I kept silent, my bones grew old through my groaning all the day long. For day and night Your hand was heavy upon me; my vitality was turned into the drought of summer. Selah*

The effect of denial is observed in the above Psalm. The author David describes the effect of his denial on his person. He states his inner being began to ache and he became depressed. He states he had a conscious knowledge his Creator's hand was upon him all the time and it was there in a disciplining fashion. It became so evident to him it drained the vitality from his inner man.

Oftentimes, the outward and obvious manifestations of denial are an increase in sensitivity to the following areas of emotion: anxiety, fear, suspicion, sarcasm, criticalness, worry, anger, laziness, melancholy, and, as previously mentioned, depression.

# Definitions of Terms

**Admit:** A person may admit to something without ever accepting responsibility for his own actions. This causes an avoidance of the reality of owning one's sin. It allows the individual to blame shift and to continue in the practice of denial and sinful habits. Examples: Cain, Balaam, King Saul, and Judas Iscariot.

**Acceptance:** When acceptance begins to bear fruit in a person's life, there is a willingness to own the problems and issues that must be dealt with and a boldness that overcomes the powerful emotions of fear, guilt, and shame. There is a newfound security and a willingness to build integrity. There is a desire to be in the light, and now the fruit of repentance has a place to grow. Examples: David, Zacchaeus, Paul, and Peter.

**John 3:21** *But he who does the truth comes to the light, that his deeds may be clearly seen, that they have been done in God.*

When there is true acceptance and repentance growing in your heart and character, you come to the light so your actions can be clearly observed. Your conscience is clean, therefore freeing you from your old suspicious or paranoid nature. With these two negative emotions eliminated from the forefront of your mind, you are now able to be confident in who you are and thus, bold and loving with your convictions.

**2 Corinthians 7:11** *For observe this very thing, that you sorrowed in a godly manner: what diligence it produced in you, what clearing of yourselves, what indignation, what fear, what vehement desire, what zeal, what vindication! In all things you proved yourselves to be clear in this matter.*

When true repentance takes root within your heart, there is a conscious awareness of sin and a deep desire to be rid of it at all cost. You begin to realize you are grieving your Lord and it harms your relationship with Him. You then are willing to do whatever it takes to repair the relationship with God and others. Godly sorrow produces repentance—which produces salvation. On your own, take some time to look up the definitions of the phrases and words listed in the above verse.

**2 Corinthians 7:9-10** *Now I rejoice, not that you were made sorry, but that your sorrow led to repentance. For you were made sorry in a godly manner, that you might suffer loss from us in nothing. For godly sorrow produces repentance leading to salvation, not to be regretted; but the sorrow of the world produces death.*

As noted here, there is a definite difference between regret and repentance. Regret is being grieved over the guilt and shame one feels from being caught and exposed by one's sin. It is unteachable and is usually "all knowed up." It says to itself, "I'll just learn how to do this (behavior) better, and the next time I won't get caught." Repentance, on the other hand, is a complete turnaround, a 180-degree turn. It is leaving the act or action completely behind and not turning back to see if it is all right or okay without you. Remember, repentance is not a turnstile! It is caused by a deep understanding of your sin through a brokenness of heart and a contrite spirit.

When repentance is given by God and growing within your heart, it recognizes that sin, no matter how big or small, deeply grieves your heavenly Father and the One who has forgiven and paid the price for your sin. An understanding begins to be established within your heart of what it cost your heavenly Father for the price to be paid in full and the precious and holy sacrifice that was provided by God Himself. You begin to understand the sacrifice completely removed the deep dark crimson stain that covered the robes you wore before Jesus' finished work upon the cross.

**Sobriety:** Sobriety is living life within a set of intrinsic limitations and accepting those limitations as a positive, rather than negative, and adapting your life to those limitations. It is experiencing a healing, to be without fear, developing wholeness and becoming well in all areas of life. It is having a life free from fear and filled with hope for the future.

Being dry is different from being sober. Being dry is simply focusing on one area of life and trying to manage it, to the harm of all the others. It is like trying to be sober by focusing on the alcohol but partaking of the flesh in other areas such as sexuality, greed, or the love of money and power. You can lack sobriety in your emotions, e.g., anger, depression, or loneliness, yet be dry or lack the influence of an intoxicant in your life and still think you are being sober. This type of action is just another form of denial.

Everything has limitations. Remember, as you practice life in your sobriety through grace you become better and better. You become well and you begin to mature. You begin to experience balance in all of life's areas. You find new freedom from your submission and surrender to Jesus. You become a new creature in Christ. Your sobriety grows from the simple knowledge of grace, to wisdom in it; from wisdom in it, to living a life of understanding through it. You become teachable, humble, meek, and contrite in heart and spirit. Grace becomes your total way of life.

**2 Corinthians 5:17** *Therefore, if anyone is in Christ, he is a new creation; old things have passed away; behold, all things have become new.*

Sobriety must always be an action. It cannot be allowed to become only a "state of being!" Sobriety embraces change. Change is not something to be afraid of but is intrinsic to sobriety. It should be grabbed with gusto and looked upon as an opportunity for good. Sobriety causes a maturing and growing up; it causes your character and actions to mellow. You are a new creation when Christ comes into your heart and life, and you can begin to identify and live out your life under a whole set of new rules and regulations. The ability to follow these rules and regulations is given by grace, which comes through faith. You will see more on this topic in lessons to come. (Romans 12:2; Ephesians 4:23-24)

## The Anniversary Periods

There are certain time periods all people with life-controlling habits must be made aware of and learn to recognize. See **The Anniversary Periods**, Appendix 5.

## The Dream Factor

Another area you need to be aware of in the early periods of sobriety is your dreams. Your newfound gift of sobriety, as well as your practice in sober living, will bring you joy beyond the boundaries of your imagination during the day. However, at times, you may find an unexpected area of confrontation that can, if allowed, rattle your cage of understanding regarding your mental state in this area of sleep. See **The Dream Factor**, Appendix 6.

## The Six R's of Recovery

The first R is <u>Recognition.</u> You must first come to the point where you recognize something is terribly wrong in your life and it is beyond your control. This serves as a severe emotional event and often is a permanent awakening. This is an event that your Conscience can no longer delay, a real-time event that you have no control over. Although this event is not always the moment that begins the repentance process, it is usually the point at which you are shaken to your core, and thus, you are never able to shake the reality of your true condition.

**Psalms 51:3** *For I acknowledge my transgressions, and my sin is always before me.*

**Psalms 73:21** *Thus my heart was grieved, and I was vexed in my mind.*

The second R is <u>Realization.</u> After recognition has a foundation within you, you must come to the point of accepting your own responsibility in the events and circumstances of your life. You must have a spiritual touch or awakening. While this process is coming to fruition, you begin to realize you must have a change in direction. This process is usually marked by several periods of self-assurance of making changes by your own will and power. While these periods are marked by failure, they serve to humble you. When this process grows into maturity, you stop blame shifting and begin to move to repentance. (Psalms 38:4, 8)

**Psalms 32:5** *I acknowledged my sin to You, and my iniquity I have not hidden. I said, "I will confess my transgressions to the LORD," and You forgave the iniquity of my sin. Selah*

The third R is <u>Repentance</u>. You have already looked at the difference between regret and repentance. After the process of recognition and realization has developed, matured, and had time to begin bearing fruit in your life, God mercifully grants you a spirit of repentance. You can then turn from your wicked ways. (2 Chronicles 7:14; Psalms 32:5; 34:18; 51:17; 2 Timothy 2:25-26)

**Joel 2:13** *So rend your heart, and not your garments; return to the LORD your God, for He is gracious and merciful, slow to anger, and of great kindness; and He relents from doing harm.*

The fourth R is <u>Receive</u>. Usually this R causes you the most discomfort because of your pride. You have to grow in this process also. Once the first three principles are firmly established, you then must learn to trust the LORD in His unfailing forgiveness and receive it. You learn how deep, how wide, how long, and how high His forgiveness is for you. When you begin to allow His forgiveness to cascade over you and to wash you clean, spotless, and blemish free, you are then able to begin the process of resting in His presence. (Proverbs 2; Proverbs 8:10-11; 10:8; Psalms 78:38-39; 103:12; Isaiah 38:17)

**Proverbs 19:20** *Listen to counsel and receive instruction, that you may be wise in your latter days.*

The fifth R is <u>Rest</u>. After receiving the ability to do the first four principles, you are now empowered to trust in God's love for you. You are given a peace that surpasses your understanding and an ability to be still. This trust gives you the ability to receive and rest in the provision that love manifests. Because of the time it took to build this foundation, you are reassured of God's continual faithfulness towards you. You are now able to look back and see the faithfulness of God in His provision for you as you have come through every trial and temptation that you have faced and conquered through Him. (Psalms 46:10; Isaiah 26:3; Philippians 4:6-7)

**Hebrews 4:9** There *remains therefore a rest for the people of God.*

The sixth and final R is <u>Restitution</u>. After the maturity and fulfillment of the previous five layers of the foundation of righteousness have been established, the fruit and manifestation of these truths are seen and observed by the actions of restitution. Restitution is the final act of repentance and contrition and is the fruit born out of a truly repentant heart.

Restitution and The Old Covenant: **Leviticus 6:2-5**, *"If a person sins and commits a trespass against the LORD by lying to his neighbor about what was delivered to him for safekeeping, or about a pledge, or about a robbery, or if he has extorted from his neighbor, or if he has found what was lost and lies concerning it, and swears falsely—in any one of these things that a man may do in which he sins: then it shall be, because he has sinned and is guilty, that he shall restore what he has stolen, or the thing which he has extorted, or what was delivered to him for safekeeping, or the lost thing which he found, or all that about which he has sworn falsely. He shall restore its full value, add one-fifth more to it, and give it to whomever it belongs, on the day of his trespass offering."* (Proverbs 6:30-31; Ezekiel 33:14-15)

Restitution—The New Covenant: Read Luke 19:1-10.

## Conclusion

As you can now see, these principles will manifest in a person whose life is truly sober and repentant and one who has a desire to have his life restored. There are no set time periods for these principles to manifest because you are all different and move at different paces. But one thing is assured – they all will take place because you have a God who is faithful and you have God's Word on it.

## Questions for Lesson 1

1. What does addiction cause to deteriorate?

2. What are the five areas you must be made aware of and sensitive to?

3. What does the natural nature of man and the fleshly or unregenerate heart of man cause?

4. What are the main areas of life that denial can affect?

5. In your own words, describe the difference between admitting and accepting.

6. In your own words, describe the difference between regret and repentance.

7. What three areas within your nature does temptation entice and effect (Appendix 5)?

8. In Appendix 1, what is the only sin you commit against the temple of God?

9. What are the 6 R's for recovery?

# Victory, Freedom, and Joy

I grew up in San Diego with wonderful parents, a couple of sisters, and we always had everything we needed. When I was in 7th grade, a deep darkness just came over me all of a sudden, with no trigger. One day I woke up and was extremely fearful. There was no reason for it that I knew of. That led into a depression, and that's where the drugs started coming in. They relieved my fears for a period of time and I just delved deeper into the hippie drug culture. I started smoking a lot of pot, dropping acid, doing speed, and all that kind of thing by 10th grade. It developed into harder and harder drugs.

I cried out to the Lord many times; I knew I needed Jesus. I wanted to come to Jesus but I thought I had to get better first. When I was about 20, I was watching Billy Graham on TV, and I remember kneeling down and just asking Jesus into my life, but by that time I was using heroin. I knew I was serious, but I had no Christian fellowship. I went right back into the life I had before.

I went through periods where I would clean up; I'd stop using for a time. There would be a new marriage, a new job, but it was the same cycle, and each time it got worse. I wasn't the out-on-the-street-drug addict for 25 years, but it ended that way. I opened doors that only God can close.

I started walking with the Lord but still had no fellowship. I started reading the Bible and really enjoyed it; it made sense. I didn't go to church; I didn't involve myself at all with other Christians. I did listen to a lot of radio programs, I'd listen every night, and I'd read my Bible every night, but after a couple of years, I fell back into the drugs. I was stealing; doing everything I could to use everyday. I was on the streets and lived the life of a major heroin addict. In August 1996, the Lord touched my heart so strong. I could just hear His voice saying, "Bill, that's enough." I had my jacket with me, and I just threw it on the ground and said, "Okay, Lord, that's it." And Praise God, that was it. It's been 10 years.

The first year I was clean I was reading the Word. I was seeking God but had no fellowship with other Christians. I was court-ordered to go to a group therapy thing. Someone there gave me a pamphlet for Pure Word. I had been listening to Pastor Bob on the radio and was interested in finding a church. I had tried a couple of churches once or twice, but just wasn't sticking with it. Anyway, I had to go; I knew I needed to break out of the isolation. So, it was almost as if the Lord said, "Come on, Bill, take a shower, come on, come to church. Let's go to this church." So I went. I went to Pure Word that first time and it was wonderful. Then I went and listened to Bob at the church and got plugged in. God just blessed me and I couldn't get enough of church, I was here every time I could be.

After all those years, through everything that had gone on in my life, the Lord brought me a wonderful wife and beautiful children. I thought there was just no way, not after all I put my body through. I have two beautiful stepchildren that I love with all my heart. I get to experience these things—it's a lot of responsibility but I never thought, I never dreamed, this would be happening to me. I don't understand how after all I've done in life. I've been so sinful, so rebellious against the Lord that He would just pour out His grace upon me, heal me, and allow me to experience victory, freedom, and joy.

God told us in His Word He has created within us the knowledge of Him. I'm confident that people who are struggling, who are in trouble, who are going through all of this, they have the knowledge of God. I would hope with that knowledge, people would stop suppressing it, stop trying to hide from God in drugs or whatever, and seek Him for who He is: a loving, wonderful, strong, compassionate Lord who is reaching out for everyone who calls upon His name.

Bill

# Lesson 2: Broken, Revealed, and Set Free, Principles 1-3

The purpose of this principle is to allow you time and fellowship in the Word of God in order to have the Holy Spirit do His divine work in you while you read and study. Remember, God's Word is alive and active! It never returns to God void but always accomplishes and prospers in that which He sent it forth to do (Hebrews 4:12; Isaiah 55:11).

If allowed to do their work, these principles will begin to work on your denial. The process of humbling and breaking will begin to take place within you. The work of the Holy Spirit is to convict you of your sin and draw you to Christ.

**Principle 1** - *I ADMIT AND ACCEPT THAT I HAVE BECOME POWERLESS OVER ALCOHOL, THE SUBSTANCE, OR SOMEONE I HAVE ABUSED AND CAUSED TO SUFFER, AND THAT MY LIFE IS UNMANAGEABLE.*

This principle states you are caught in a lifestyle of sin and fear. You are not only powerless over the substance(s) you have abused, but, if left to yourself, you are not capable of managing your own life without help from God. The following scriptures and definitions show you that, without the LORD to manage your life, you will never obtain any real measure of peace or happiness.

The beginning point in your walk in sobriety has to be the place of recognizing that all are sinners and that there is only one way to God – not many as you have heard. God desires a living and loving relationship with mankind. But man, because of his fallen nature, desires to be religious. God desires to make the pathway to Him straight and narrow for man. However, because of pride, man desires to set up his own set of rules, regulations, rituals, and ceremonies to obtain and gain entrance to heaven. You have to come to an end of yourself before you will allow God to save you. The following principles and selected scriptures will show you your need and your behaviors before Christ is able to enter your heart and becomes LORD of your life.

## Broken

**Galatians 5:19-21** *Now the works of the flesh are evident, which are: adultery, fornication, uncleanness, lewdness, idolatry, sorcery, hatred, contentions, jealousies, outbursts of wrath, selfish ambitions, dissensions, heresies, envy, murders, drunkenness, revelries, and the like; of which I tell you beforehand, just as I also told you in time past, that those who practice such things will not inherit the kingdom of God.*

Without God's divine authorship in your life, you are lost, helpless, and inadequate to overcome the sin in your life. This verse states your works, acts, or deeds are evident or obvious. Your denial will convince you, despite the damage it does to your conscience, as well as to others, to ignore the fact that you are doing wrong. To prevent any misunderstanding, the definitions of the manifestations of the flesh are listed below. Greek translations for the words are in parentheses.

1. *Adultery* (moicheia): sexual unfaithfulness to husband or wife. It is also looking on a woman or a man to lust after her or him. Looking at and lusting after the opposite sex whether in person, magazines, books, on beaches or anywhere else is adultery. Imagining and lusting within the heart is the very same as committing the act.

2. *Fornication* (porneia): a broad word including all forms of immoral and sexual acts. It is pre-marital sex and adultery; it is abnormal sex, all kinds of sexual vice.

3. *Uncleanness* (akatharsia): moral impurity; doing things that dirty, pollute, and soil life.

4. *Lasciviousness* (aselgeia): filthiness, indecency, shamelessness. A chief characteristic of the behavior is open and shameless indecency. It means unrestrained evil thoughts and behavior. It is giving in to brutish and lustful desires, a readiness for any pleasure. It is a man who knows no restraint, a man who has sinned so much that he no longer cares what people say or think. It is something far more distasteful than just doing wrong. The man who misbehaves usually tries to hide his wrong, but a lascivious man does not care who knows about his exploits or shame. He wants; therefore, he seeks to take and gratify. Decency and opinion do not matter. Initially when he began to sin, he did as all men do: he misbehaved in secret. But eventually, the sin got the best of him—to the point that he no long cared who saw or knew. He became the subject of a master—the master of habit, of the thing itself. Men become the slaves of such things as unbridled lust, wantonness, licentiousness, outrageousness, shamelessness, insolence (Mk. 7:22), wanton manners, filthy words, indecent body movements, immoral handling of males and females (Rom. 13:13), public display of affection, carnality, gluttony, and sexual immorality (1 Pet. 4:3; 2 Pet. 2:2, 18). (Compare 2 Cor. 12:21; Gal. 5:19; Eph. 4:19; 2 Pet. 2:7.)

5. *Idolatry* (eidololatreia): the worship of idols, whether mental or made by man's hands; the worship of some idea of what God is like, of an image of God within a person's mind; the giving of one's primary devotion (time and energy) to something other than God.

6. *Witchcraft* (pharmakeia): sorcery; the use of drugs or of evil spirits to gain control over the lives of others or over one's own life. In the present context it would include all forms of seeking the control of one's fate including astrology, palm reading, séances, fortune telling, crystals, and other forms of witchcraft.

7. *Hatred* (echthrai): enmity, hostility, and animosity. It is the hatred that lingers and is held for a long, long time; a hatred that is deep within.

8. *Variance* (eris): strife, discord, contention, fighting, struggling, quarreling, dissension, wrangling. It means that a man fights against another person in order to get something: position, promotion, property, honor, and recognition. He deceives, doing whatever has to be done to get what he is after.

9. **Emulations** (zeloi): jealousy, wanting and desiring to have what someone else has. It may be material things, recognition, honor, or position.

10. **Wrath** (thumoi): bursts of anger; indignation; a violent, explosive temper; quick-tempered explosive reactions that arise from stirred and boiling emotions. But it is anger which fades away just as quickly as it arose. It is not anger that lasts.

11. **Strife** (eritheiai): conflict, struggle, fight, contention, faction, dissension; a party spirit, a cliquish spirit.

12. **Seditions** (dichostasiai): division, rebellion, standing against others, splitting off from others.

13. **Heresies** (aireseis): rejecting the fundamental beliefs of God, Christ, the Scriptures, and the church; believing and holding to some teaching other than the truth.

14. **Envyings** (phthonoi): this word goes beyond jealousy. It is the spirit...
—that wants not only the things that another person has, but begrudges the fact that the person has them.
—that wants not only the things to be taken away from the person, but wants him to suffer through the loss of them.

15. **Murders** (phonoi): to kill, to take the life of another person. Murder is sin against the sixth commandment.

16. **Drunkenness** (methai): taking drink or drugs to affect one's senses for lust or pleasure; becoming tipsy or intoxicated; partaking of drugs; seeking to loosen moral restraint for bodily pleasure.

17. **Revellings** (komoi): carousing; uncontrolled license, indulgence, and pleasure; taking part in wild parties or in drinking parties; lying around indulging in feeding the lusts of the flesh; orgies.

The following are further examples of the above definitions from the NIV: adultery (sexual immorality), uncleanness (impurity), lasciviousness (debauchery), wrath (fits of rage), strife (selfish ambition), seditions (dissensions), and heresies (factions).

From this list of definitions, you can identify with at least a couple, if not all, in one form or another. You have done some of these at least a time or two. Some you have practiced until they have affected your character and have become your habit.

**Romans 6:23** *For the wages of sin is death, but the gift of God is eternal life in Christ Jesus our Lord.*

Whenever you are tempted to do your own thing or have a god of your own understanding, you are in sin. There is an inevitable wage that must be paid upon death. God states you can pay it yourself, or He offers to pay it for you by offering His one and only Son in the place of your sins. You must confront the idea and accept the fact you have sinned against the LORD by trying to control your own destiny and offer up to Him your works.

**Isaiah 55:8-9** *"For My thoughts are not your thoughts, nor are your ways My ways," says the LORD. "For as the heavens are higher than the earth, so are My ways higher than your ways and My thoughts than your thoughts."*

God and the law demand that you be holy, loving, and perfect, without exception. Perfection is the only way God can fellowship with you; this is His nature and character. It is not because He is uptight and cranky. Sin cannot be found before Him. You cannot be God's counselor or advisor. He doesn't need your help, and you certainly don't fit in the seat of His throne. (Isaiah 40:13; Romans 11:34)

**Romans 3:10, 23** *As it is written: "There is none righteous, no, not one…," …for all have sinned and fall short of the glory of God,…*

These scriptures show <u>all</u> of mankind is in sin and there are no exceptions. Your denial causes you to rationalize that somehow God could overlook smaller sins but such is not the case. Your denial causes you to measure God's holiness according to your standards, which always change according to the whims of your emotions or circumstances. God, on the other hand, never changes (Malachi 3:6; Hebrews 13:8).

**James 2:10** *For whoever shall keep the whole law, and yet stumble in one point, he is guilty of all.*

James points out if you break the law in just one point, you are guilty of breaking it all.

Also, take note that your good works can never add up to the point of outweighing or tipping the scale so they balance out the weight of your sins. In fact, God states this important point about your good works. **Isaiah 64:6,** *"But we are all like an unclean thing, and all our righteousnesses are like filthy rags; we all fade as a leaf, and our iniquities, like the wind, have taken us away."*

Denial causes you to think that in your maturity or old age you now are able somehow to keep the whole law. The older you get, the more you put the weight of your confidence on your good works. You forget that while growing up you broke the law all the time. Now as an older person you have just grown more refined in your denial and sin. In fact, you were conceived in sin, and from the womb, you were rebellious, stubborn, and demanded your own way. (Psalms 51:5, 58:3; Isaiah 48:8; Jeremiah 13:23)

To prove this point, think about this for a moment and ask yourself this question. Did you ever go to school to learn to lie, cheat, steal, envy, hate, covet, swear, or learn to love yourself? Is there such a school where you send your infants and children to learn these fine skills? When do you graduate? Can you earn a degree in these? Are we all guilty of these sins? The answer is obvious, isn't it?

When the process of the breakdown of your denial begins, your conscience is often at a heightened awareness of being. The doorway to your conscience is usually opened when you experience pain in your life or when you incur a cost to your pocketbook. As stated in Lesson 1, if the life areas of health, social, or family have no impact on your denial or conscience, usually the legal area of your life does. When you start to have problems in the legal area, the impact of the reality of the judge, prosecutor, and people who you are involved with through the experiences of jails or court-ordered classes, makes you realize something is going wrong because you think you are better than this.

**Romans 2:14-15** *…for when Gentiles, who do not have the law, by nature do the things in the law, these, although not having the law, are a law to themselves, who show the work of the law written in their hearts, their conscience also bearing witness, and between themselves their thoughts accusing or else excusing them)…*

This verse shows once your conscience is touched and the doorway to your heart is slightly opened, the work of God can begin to take place. A severe emotional event can now transpire. These scriptures point out that God has been trying to show you from the very beginning that you would have a choice to obey Him or rebel against Him. Compare with Romans 7:13, especially the last part of the verse. (Genesis 4:7; James 4:17)

The conscience is a sense of what is right or wrong in one's thoughts, actions, or motives. It is the discerning tool for right and wrong. The work of the conscience is independent and direct. Conscience is not to be confused with your ability to reason. Before regeneration, your reasoning often overrides your conscience and helps you to justify your sinful behavior. You see the important work of your conscience and the need of having one in the following references from Romans. Please remember the will has to be consciously opened to the desire and temptation at this point in order to be affected.

**Romans 7:18-19, 23** *For I know that in me (that is, in my flesh) nothing good dwells; for to will is present with me, but how to perform what is good I do not find. For the good that I will to do, I do not do; but the evil I will not to do, that I practice…. But I see another law in my members, warring against the law of my mind, and bringing me into captivity to the law of sin which is in my members.*

The battle raging here is between the conscience and the lustful desires within the body. Remember the word of your LORD when He stated, **Mark 14:38**, *"Watch and pray, lest you enter into temptation. The spirit indeed is willing, but the flesh is weak."* This points out the truth that the part of you that is the strongest is the part of you that will rule. If your focus is on worldly things and the flesh, that's the part that will be the strongest. If the things of the Spirit are where your focus is, your will should be lined up with the will of the Father and Christ. (Romans 8:5)

**Romans 7:24-25** *O wretched man that I am! Who will deliver me from this body of death? I thank God—through Jesus Christ our Lord! So then, with the mind I myself serve the law of God, but with the flesh the law of sin.*

From these verses you can clearly see the inner struggle that takes place within you. It is humbling to know there is nothing good dwelling within you and all your works, which you consider righteous, are like filthy rags in God's sight (Isaiah 64:6).

As you come to the end of this principle, your heart has been prepared for the next step, which is a willingness to accept there is a possibility you don't have all the answers.

# Revealed

**Principle 2 -** *I BEGIN TO BELIEVE THAT THROUGH JESUS CHRIST I CAN BE RESTORED TO A RIGHT RELATIONSHIP WITH GOD THE FATHER AND SUBSEQUENT SANITY AND STABILITY IN MY LIFE.*

This principle talks about your coming to believe you can have a right relationship with God the Father. As you look at those who have this relationship with God, their lives seem to be so much happier than the lives of those who don't. The question you may be asking yourself is, "Will God really work in my life if I do believe?" The answer is definitely "yes"—He is only waiting for you to give Him the opportunity. This principle will help you to better understand and to believe Jesus has provided a way for you to have this relationship with God and all the benefits that result from it. God has done everything possible to provide you a way to come to Him and receive life abundantly.

This principle addresses the fact that the lifestyle you have been living was one that caused you to live outside of or beside yourself, resulting in your insanity. It means if you had been of a sober mind, you would never have participated in or thought of the behaviors that now cause you shame. Let's start with a revealing look at God's heart for you. **Jeremiah 31:3**, *"The LORD has appeared of old to me, saying: 'Yes, I have loved you with an everlasting love; therefore with lovingkindness I have drawn you.'"* Reflect on this scripture's meaning, as well as what it shows God's desire for mankind truly is. (Isaiah 1:17-20; Revelation 3:20; Romans 10:13; John 10:10; 2 Peter 3:9)

**John 14:1, 6** *"Let not your heart be troubled; you believe in God, believe also in Me."…. Jesus said to him, "I am the way, the truth, and the life. No one comes to the Father except through Me."*

The secondary focus of this principle is to confront your behavior and denial and to draw your heart to the area of belief. You have the ability and free will to believe in a variety of things. The scriptures make it very clear the one thing you don't believe in is the one and only true God. In the world there are many different beliefs and an abundance of gods. Jesus told you there is only one way to God, and when confronted with what your carnal nature (flesh) deems restricted, narrow minded, or fundamental, you are often offended. Belief in God is much more than just being intellectual; it requires a restful work called faith. Jesus explains His desire is for you not only to believe in God, but also in Him. Jesus also points out He is the only way to the Father.

Read John 3:3-6. Jesus reveals the truth. Even though Nicodemus is a devout and religious man, a very pious Pharisee, and Israel's teacher (John 3:10), he still cannot enter the kingdom of God. It takes a supernatural event, a rebirth, and just like your birth, you have nothing to do with it. It takes God!

**Romans 8:9-11** *But you are not in the flesh but in the Spirit, if indeed the Spirit of God dwells in you. Now if anyone does not have the Spirit of Christ, he is not His. And if Christ is in you, the body is dead because of sin, but the Spirit is life because of righteousness. But if the Spirit of Him who raised Jesus from the dead dwells in you, He who raised Christ from the dead will also give life to your mortal bodies through His Spirit who dwells in you.*

These closing verses for Principle 2 are from the letter to the Romans. If you are "born again," you are transformed from the nature of Adam to the nature of Christ. You'll notice the very important two-letter words "if." If you have been born again and redeemed in Christ, you don't have to worry about your works or what you have to do for Him. There will be a change because He has made all things new, and you will begin to have a change in your desires. Paul states if you are found in Christ, your mortal body is dead because of sin, meaning sin is now powerless to rule over you. Sin is now a choice for those in Christ. You have been set free from this body of death, and the Holy Spirit now lives and rules in you. He has given you a righteous heart and a life that desires to follow the precepts of God. It is literally the fulfillment of Ezekiel 36:26-27. You now participate in the resurrection life of the Son of God. You are lifted up and out of the main current of the world so you are no longer a slave to the world and your lusts, but are now a slave unto righteousness.

## Set Free

**Principle 3 - *I MAKE A DECISION TO TURN MY LIFE AND MY WILL FROM THE THINGS OF THE PAST AND INVITE JESUS TO BE LORD, SAVIOR, AND MANAGER OF MY LIFE.***

In Principle 1, you admitted and accepted your life was unmanageable. In Principle 2, you came to believe Jesus was God Incarnate. Now it's time to do something about that belief and that is, to turn your life and your will over to Him completely. You are tired of playing God, and you have decided to let your Creator, who is Jesus Christ, become LORD of your life. You humbly ask Him to forgive your sins, come into your heart, and be the LORD and Manager of your life. You realize now you need a Savior and need His help from this day forward to live and do His will, instead of your own. The study of this principle will help you to discover the foundation of this truth for your life.

**Matthew 11:28-30** *Come to Me, all you who labor and are heavy laden, and I will give you rest. Take My yoke upon you and learn from Me, for I am gentle and lowly in heart, and you will find rest for your souls. For My yoke is easy and My burden is light.*

As you examine this important process, the evidence of your surrender is your willingness to go to the LORD. You don't turn to other things; this time you turn to Him. Remember, the life of Jesus was a life of attraction—not promotion. The benefits He showers upon you after your surrender are nothing short of phenomenal. He tells you His way of life is not a burden to follow or imitate and you will find rest for your soul. What a promise! Lastly, in Matthew 11, you see that a fruitful walk in the LORD is sweat-free and simple. The formula is this: God's Love + Grace + Mercy = Forgiveness and Abundant Life.

**Proverbs 16:1-3**, *The preparations of the heart belong to man, but the answer of the tongue is from the LORD. All the ways of a man are pure in his own eyes, but the LORD weighs the spirits. Commit your works to the LORD, and your thoughts will be established.*

More evidence of your free will is listed in this verse. God states you are free to plan your way, but your answers are from Him. It tells you that until you are delivered from yourself, all your ways seem right in your own eyes, in your own understanding. The LORD has to weigh your spirit; He has to search you and be allowed to lead and convict you. He is the only one who can make you committed, steadfast, consistent, and sufficient. Only then can you operate in the mind of Christ, and your mind is renewed and transformed daily. (Ephesians 2:10)

After your mind is renewed and transformed, you are then enabled to perform the will of God in and through your daily walk. The following verse illustrates this truth for you.

**2 Corinthians 6:2** *For He says: "In an acceptable time I have heard you, and in the day of salvation I have helped you." Behold, now is the accepted time; behold, now is the day of salvation.*

This verse states there is an appointed time for salvation. It is hard to understand because, according to this verse, it is appropriated by both God and your free will. God uses all things to help you obtain the understanding of your need for salvation, including all your iniquities, transgressions, and sins. At the fruition of this period of time, the need of salvation is recognized. Your will is surrendered and yielded to Him, and the new birth in Christ takes place within you.

**John 3:36** *He who believes in the Son has everlasting life; and he who does not believe the Son shall not see life, but the wrath of God abides on him.*

Jesus tells you belief in Him affects your conscience and your actions to the point you are able to entrust Him with your life. Faith in Him changes your knowledge and understanding of Him. Faith suddenly helps you to see and understand the things that are unseen and helps you to let go of the things you see and value. You now have a change in the perspective of your reality, the values of your treasures, and those things you count as important.

**Romans 10:9-10** *…that if you confess with your mouth the Lord Jesus and believe in your heart that God has raised Him from the dead, you will be saved. For with the heart one believes unto righteousness, and with the mouth confession is made unto salvation.*

The results of this new perspective and foundation of faith are heard in the confession of your mouth and change of your speech. The meaning of confession simply means you agree with God about any subject, that He is right. With the change of your heart, you are now able to believe in the need of salvation. Because of this change, you begin to have a desire to preach and tell others about it.

**1 John 5:4-5** *For whatever is born of God overcomes the world. And this is the victory that has overcome the world—our faith. Who is he who overcomes the world, but he who believes that Jesus is the Son of God?*

The faith God gives you is manifested in such a way you begin to appropriate it in ways that go beyond your logic's ability or strength to understand. It allows you to rest and be still when everything else is going wrong around you. Faith allows you to know the eye of the lover of your soul and His mighty hand surrounds you during the time of trial or tribulation. Faith becomes the power that propels you into action. That action becomes the works that others see. The result is—you are transformed into an overcomer.

**John 12:24** *Most assuredly, I say to you, unless a grain of wheat falls into the ground and dies, it remains alone; but if it dies, it produces much grain.*

In this verse, you see a mystery about a seed. This is absolute truth and one that defies worldly logic. How can life come from death? You can find another example of what Jesus meant in John 3:6. The flesh cannot bring about the resurrection life you so desperately need. It also shows you the proof of a grace-filled reward that happens in a Christian's life. You have nothing to do with your being born, your life and what it comprises, the work of salvation, or the rewards you will receive in heaven. Grace could be explained in the following ways.

Grace has promised to <u>do</u>. It does what you cannot do. Its yoke is not burdensome or heavy. It is light. It not only gives you life, but also develops it within you. Grace births you and causes you to grow. It forgives you and transforms you. It causes you to be humble and keeps you that way. It gives you faith and causes that faith to develop and grow in strength and boldness. Grace teaches you the truth that <u>you can't</u>, but <u>God can</u>.

Grace can also be explained like this. God gives you faith, He causes you to believe, He causes you to walk, and He then calls you and gives you your assignments. He enables you to accomplish what He has assigned and provides you with the power and the obedience to complete it. <u>He does it all!</u> He then rewards you as though you did it on your own. What wonderful good news!

Jesus told you if you desire to follow Him you must deny (die to) yourself, daily pick up the instrument of your death (the Cross), and follow Him (be humble, teachable, yielded, and surrendered). This means you are dead in the flesh (to your sinful nature) and alive to Him in the spirit. He has control over all. He is the LORD of the harvest and His Father is the vinedresser (John 15:1, 4).

**2 Corinthians 5:15-19** *... and He died for all, that those who live should live no longer for themselves, but for Him who died for them and rose again. Therefore, from now on, we regard no one according to the flesh. Even though we have known Christ according to the flesh, yet now we know Him thus no longer. Therefore, if anyone is in Christ, he is a new creation; old things have passed away; behold, all things have become new. Now all things are of God, who has reconciled us to Himself through Jesus Christ, and has given us the ministry of reconciliation, that is, that God was in Christ reconciling the world to Himself, not imputing their trespasses to them, and has committed to us the word of reconciliation.*

These verses illustrate for you the main aspects of a transformed life. Paul tells you if a transformation has taken place within you, you will be changed from the inside first, emanating outward like ripples from a pebble tossed into a mirror-surfaced pond in the morning.

Paul tells you Jesus died for all, and because of your reception of this new life, you are now enabled to live for Him and others. This means before Jesus enters a person's life, he is a slave to self-centeredness. He is not able to be unselfish. On the other hand, when the redeemed life of a Christian takes place and develops, a new perspective is birthed. The eyes of the heart are opened and the new life begins to mature. You begin to see the freedom found in serving others.

Paul then tells you that you no longer regard people according to the flesh. This means you no longer examine the person's actions from a human perspective, but in a Christ-like perspective. You now have the ability to look at action done in the flesh through eyes of LOVE. You are now enabled to separate the sin from the sinner. You are now able to be patient with others because of the understanding you have received from Christ. He is very longsuffering with you, and it is this longsuffering that brought you to Him (Romans 2:4). He also states you are now able to understand the mysteries of the Gospel where before your new birth, you were unable to understand (1 Corinthians 2:14). Because of this new ability, you know a new birth has occurred and old things have passed away.

In the final verse you are told the reasons why you now have a desire to reconcile with others. Again, this is not from you but from God. It is a supernatural result of your new birth in Christ.

**1 Peter 1:13-16** *Therefore gird up the loins of your mind, be sober, and rest your hope fully upon the grace that is to be brought to you at the revelation of Jesus Christ; 14 as obedient children, not conforming yourselves to the former lusts, as in your ignorance; 15 but as He who called you is holy, you also be holy in all your conduct,16 because it is written, "Be holy, for I am holy."*

You see the importance of protecting your mind and allowing Christ to change your being. You see the beginning process of the change that takes place within you. Change isn't change until it is change. You have your words, thoughts, and actions transformed by Him.

Peter tells you first to protect your mind. He instructs you to gird up the loins of your mind. This was the place where the Hebrews thought the generative power (semen) resided. In other words, this is the birthing place for ideas and thoughts. It should be a holy place, one where life and peace are birthed, not death and sin. You are to be mindful of the need to take captive your thought life and not let it run wild. Paul told you the same thing in 2 Corinthians 10:5. This also means you are mentally to prepare for battle and action as a Christian. He instructs you to be sober, this means to be balanced (calm and collected in spirit), temperate, dispassionate, and circumspect. He tells you that you are to rest your hope fully upon the grace that was brought to you upon the revelation of Jesus Christ. This means you are to trust in the abilities of your LORD, not yourself, to bring about the completion of this wonderful work of sobriety He has begun.

Verse 14 describes what hope can do for you if you are willing to allow the LORD to fulfill His will within you. You are told that hope stirs a desire within you to obey as children do. This describes innocence. Children believe without pretense or reservation. With your mind alert and sober, you are then able to rest in the grace God has lavished upon you so you can believe in a childlike fashion. If you have the faith of a child, you are then able to appropriate this trust in a strength that causes you to put off the old man and its former behaviors and ignorance.

In verses 15 and 16, you are taught God is holy. Because of your new birth, you have a new character and nature within you that now can be in control. The old man is crucified with Christ and the new man is alive to God (Galatians 2:19-20). You are enabled to begin to practice living a life that is pleasing to God. Because of the work of God within you, you are now able to live a life above the standard of the world. You are now holy, just as the Lord God is holy.

## Conclusion

**1 Peter 3:16** ...*having a good conscience, that when they defame you as evildoers, those who revile your good conduct in Christ may be ashamed.* (Compare with John 8:9; Acts 24:16; Romans 2:15; 9:1; 1 Corinthians 8:12; 10:23-33; and 1 Timothy 4:2.)

As you close this principle, you are made aware of the power of your conscience and the necessity of having a clean one before God. If your conscience is not clean and at rest, it has the ability to split the work of God into two different directions. You cannot be doubled-minded (James 1:6-8). As you have already observed, the work of the conscience has to be guided by the Spirit of God. You need the healing touch of God within your conscience in order to proceed with a life of liberty and sobriety.

Your past behaviors caused you to ignore your conscience and it had been damaged to the point of almost severing it, in some cases. But by the grace and mercy of God, you are able to have your conscience healed. By having a clean conscience you are able to withstand the persecution that will come (Luke 6:22; John 15:18). You now have a balanced and right perspective on the things that happen to you because the eyes of your heart are open to the reality of what is truly real. Because of this new steadfastness, you are now strong enough in your resolve to bless those who persecute you and to remain focused on what your goal is—to finish or complete the cleansing of your conscience in the light of Christ. This brings about condemnation and shame on those who are still in darkness and sin.

You are now ready to proceed on to Principle 4 and have God search you and reveal to you what He considers sinful and unclean.

# Questions for Lesson 2

## Principle 1

1.  What is the purpose of this lesson? What will it accomplish if allowed to complete its work?

2.  In the list of the obvious acts, works, or deeds of the sinful nature, otherwise known as the flesh, which of these can you most identify with? List them. What have you done to try to control them?

3.  If you have a god of your own understanding, what are you controlled by: the Spirit of God or your sinful nature?

4.  What function does the conscience perform within you? What causes you to realize you have a problem?

5.  (Principle 2) You have the ability and free will to believe in a variety of things and there are many different beliefs and an abundance of gods in this world to believe in. Belief in God though is much more than just being intellectual. Why did Jesus tell you there was only one way to God and what was it?

6.  If you didn't have any choice in your original birth, isn't it a wonder you do in your second? Jesus told you that you had the power to give birth to flesh but only the Spirit had the ability to give birth to the Spirit. What does this say about your ability to understand God? See Romans 8:5-8; 1 Corinthians 2:14.

7.  (Principle 3) Why does it take a decision and the exercising of your will to turn your life over to Jesus Christ? Why doesn't Jesus just force Himself into your heart?

8. In John 3:36 you are told if you believe in Jesus Christ as the one and only begotten Son, you will have and be given everlasting life. Why is faith the key and not your works?

9. How are you transformed into "overcomers"?

10. How does a seed illustrate for you your lack of control or ability to change yourself?

# Searching for God

When I met my wife Gina at an AA meeting, we were both reeling from failed marriages, shattered dreams, and struggling with many sinful life-controlling issues. One of the most prominent was drug and alcohol abuse. We had both been to treatment centers in the past. We were told to find a god of our own understanding, trust in others who were struggling with the same issues, and "work some steps." That worked for a little while but soon we were both back to our old comfortable habits of using drugs and struggling to make a life together.

Our lives were so empty and unfulfilled. As time went on, we started growing further and further apart. Gina started down that long road into a dark depression and I continued to lie, cheat, and steal as our life began to unravel. Finally, after 27 years of drug use, we lost everything and I landed in prison. Gina found herself incarcerated for a short period of time then thrust back out to go it alone.

I now had time to take a hard look at my life. I did not like what I saw. Doing things on my own, I had failed as a father, husband, son, and friend. I was unkind, selfish, prideful, and dishonest. I took advantage of everyone around me and blamed others for my mistakes.

I taught drug and alcohol classes at the prison. It was easy; I had done drugs for most of my life. It was during this time I realized there had to be something more. If not, I was doomed. I turned to God and asked Him to become the Lord of my life and to help me change—from the inside. Only He could change my heart in order for me to become a new person.

When I was released, I was reunited with Gina who had continued to struggle in a godless life while I was gone. God used me to show her what a profound change He could make in a person. We began going to Pure Word meetings. The Lord softened and changed her heart. We fellowshipped with godly people who had come from the same place we had. God put joy in our life and began to show us how truly wonderful life could be. He provided for our needs and made it possible for us to help others. God changed us so completely people find it hard to believe we lived like we did. With Christ, we now live the life we both had always dreamed of but never thought possible. Although six years has gone by, the memory of living life without Christ remains fresh in our minds, always reminding us constantly to be thankful for God's saving grace.

Greg

# Lesson 3: The Importance of a God Search, Principle 4

You now have a newfound security and relationship with the LORD due to your new knowledge of His love for you and your surrender to Him. Now you are ready to proceed with the process of taking an inventory or better identified as a God search.

When you allow God to do the searching, you can be secure and at peace. You are able to be still before Him like a patient before a surgeon. You trust His hand to hold the scalpel, and you trust Him to know how to use it for the purpose it was designed. You trust His diagnosis and knowledge of the problem. You trust the process it will take for the necessary healing to take place in your soul.

As you go through these selected scriptures, you will see the importance of allowing God to search you and know you. Without His help, you would be unforgiven and hopelessly lost. Through the power of the Holy Spirit and the cleansing of His Word, you find the mercy and compassion needed to continue this process for sobriety. You also begin to appropriate the necessary faith that brings healing, security, and hope for the future by obeying His instructions and following His examples listed in scripture.

**Principle 4 -** *WITH THE HELP OF THE HOLY SPIRIT, I HUMBLY, BOLDLY, AND COURAGEOUSLY ASK HIM TO SEARCH ME AND REVEAL TO ME THE TRUE CONDITION OF MY HEART, TO SHOW ME MY ANXIETIES OR FEARS, AND POINT OUT TO ME MY SIN AGAINST GOD AND OTHERS IN MY LIFE. ONLY WITH HIS HELP CAN I KNOW FOR SURE, AND IN ALL TRUTH, THE EXACT NATURE OF MY SIN.*

Once you accept Jesus as LORD of your life, He gives you the desire to start housecleaning. In Principle 4, the process of becoming more of what He wants you to become begins by taking a fearless personal inventory, which is recognizing where you have fallen short of His standards in your life.

The first thing to do is to agree with God and His identifications of your sins. Next, you identify if these sins are still ongoing and the amount of damage sin has done in your life and the lives that surround you. One of the most helpful things to do is to write these sins down so you begin to become accountable, first to God, then to others. As you do this, you will be encouraged by His grace, mercy, and faithfulness towards you as you die to yourself, pick up your cross daily, and follow Jesus, your LORD. The witness of this growth will prepare you to continue on with Principles 5, 6, and 7.

**Psalms 139:23-24** *Search me, O God, and know my heart; try me, and know my anxieties; and see if there is any wicked way in me, and lead me in the way everlasting.*

These scriptures are from the God-empowered heart of King David. He had already poured out his heart in confession to the LORD and desired to have the LORD search him after what he felt was his full confession. This verse shows you that even after you think you have done a thorough job of agreeing with God about your sin against Him and others, you still need His stamp of approval upon your confession. You need to know your conscience and heart have been cleansed by your LORD's blood and rest with full assurance there is no foothold remaining the enemy can use against you. Notice David asks the LORD to reveal his own heart to him and to show him his anxieties or fears. What place do fears play in your inability to complete this principle? How much courage does it take to face yourself in the mirror and accept the responsibility of all your actions?

David finishes with the request to be led. He shows the humility and desire to follow after the Master proceeds <u>after</u> God cleanses you and frees you from guilt, shame, and condemnation. This is the manifestation of faith through trust in God, which is the proof of your faith through the Godly works you now perform in the light of His love.

**1 John 1:8** *If we say that we have no sin, we deceive ourselves, and the truth is not in us.*

**Proverbs 20:9** *Who can say, "I have made my heart clean, I am pure from my sin"?*

These two scriptures show how man can deceive himself by thinking he has no sin. John states two important things. The first is if you say you have no sin, you are deceived or in denial. The second is more poignant and that is—truth is not in you. The truth sheds light on your heart and soul and it reveals and exposes the darkness within them. The scriptures also point out just knowing the word brings about nothing. See John 5:39; 1 Corinthians 8:1b-2; and James 1:22.

You might do good works and think you have done a thorough job of cleansing yourself, but scripture points out even your works of righteousness are like filthy rags to God if done in your own understanding (Job 15:14-16; Isaiah 64:6). Only the blood of Jesus has the power to cleanse you of all your sins, and only it can keep your conscience free from condemnation (Hebrews 10:22).

**Psalms 19:12-14** *Who can understand his errors? Cleanse me from secret faults. Keep back Your servant also from presumptuous sins; let them not have dominion over me. Then I shall be blameless, and I shall be innocent of great transgression. Let the words of my mouth and the meditation of my heart be acceptable in Your sight, O LORD, my strength and my Redeemer.*

David writes he is unable to discern or understand with his mind (i.e., emotions and soul) all the ways and consequences of his mistakes. He openly requests of God to cleanse him from his secret faults. These are not secrets he has consciously kept from God (compare with 1 Corinthians 2:11), but secrets that are kept deep within him, in his subconscious. Remember the words of the Lord spoken to Jeremiah in **Jeremiah 17:9-10**, *"The heart is deceitful above all things, and desperately wicked; who can know it? I the LORD, search the heart, I test the mind, even to give every man according to his ways, according to the fruit of his doings."* David also asks God to keep him from sins that are presumptuous, that is, sins that are arrogant, proud, and boldly disrespectful. David also acknowledges these sins have the ability to capture him and cause him to surrender and become a slave to them. He states if God answers this request, he shall be blameless and pure. Once the heart is cleansed, the mouth responds with words of purity, and it is able to concentrate on the goodness of God. Because the Word creates within you the Godly humility and contrite heart God requires, you are now enabled to rely on the strength of God and His redemption. You are now able to surrender your control and rely on His.

**Mark 7:20-23** *And He said, "What comes out of a man, that defiles a man. For from within, out of the heart of men, proceed evil thoughts, adulteries, fornications, murders, thefts, covetousness, wickedness, deceit, lewdness, an evil eye, blasphemy, pride, foolishness. All these evil things come from within and defile a man."*

Jesus states the root of your problem is not outside of you but within you. He clearly states your problem is your heart. These thoughts and actions could be an addition to the list of the manifested works of the flesh Paul lists in his letter to the Galatians. They clearly affect your thoughts, words, and actions. Only the Holy Spirit can reveal these areas of defect within your character, and after the revelation, only He can heal your broken and contrite spirit, putting you back together again.

**Romans 6:16** *Do you not know that to whom you present yourselves slaves to obey, you are that one's slaves whom you obey, whether of sin leading to death, or of obedience leading to righteousness?*

Paul defines for you the process of carnal bondage. This is the scriptural definition of addiction. Paul shows you when you surrender your will to the object of your desire, you become entangled and enslaved to it. It also shows you the power of your choices. Please take note of the following verses: 1 Corinthians 6:12, 10:23; and 2 Corinthians 6:12.

**Galatians 5:13-18** *For you, brethren, have been called to liberty; only do not use liberty as an opportunity for the flesh, but through love serve one another. 14 For all the law is fulfilled in one word, even in this: "You shall love your neighbor as yourself." 15 But if you bite and devour one another, beware lest you be consumed by one another! 16 I say then: Walk in the Spirit, and you shall not fulfill the lust of the flesh. 17 For the flesh lusts against the Spirit, and the Spirit against the flesh; and these are contrary to one another, so that you do not do the things that you wish. 18 But if you are led by the Spirit, you are not under the law.*

Your marching orders are given here. You have been called to liberty, not slavery; you have the power to choose. You are commanded to love one another, but you still have a choice to obey or rebel. Remember the periphery or boundary of liberty is the law and bondage.

You also see the value of having a correct focus. You are given two choices—either a horizontal or a vertical focus. If you focus on self or man and his doings, you will have a limited horizontal perspective, which becomes full of hopelessness. If you focus on Christ (vertical focus) as you are instructed to do by the scriptures, He will give you an unlimited perspective and a vision full of hope.

The whole law is summed up in one word—love. You should love your neighbor as much as you already love yourself. How much do you love yourself? Well, that is how much you are to love your neighbor. In verse 15, you see the graphic results of conflict if you don't love. Tragedies result from broken relationships, and they prove the scriptures don't lie. They prove anything brought about by your flesh will not last.

In verse 16, you see a change of focus and Paul begins to instruct you in the ministry and available power of the Holy Spirit. He tells you to <u>walk in the Spirit</u>. This means you are to live, to be filled with, to move, to progress and mature, to regulate one's life, and to conduct and control one's self through the regulation and guidance of the Holy Spirit. At the moment you are regenerated and redeemed, you are able to lay aside the old man and his nature. You are told in the scriptures your new life and faith in Christ gives you the ability to choose between which nature you will yield to—the flesh or the Spirit. You are now enabled to show your love through obedience to Christ and put aside your old man and his ways. Read Romans 6:6, 6:11-12; Ephesians 4:22-24; and Colossians 3:5-11.

In verse 17, there is an illustration of the mental struggle you will experience as you learn and practice putting off the old man and his patterned thought process. You are habitual in your thinking process. As a "born again" Christian, you now have to exercise and practice a new way of living. Because of the ability to choose now, you can leave behind the old man and his ways. See Galatians 5:24; Romans 13:14; and Colossians 2:11.

Jesus desires to pour you into a new wine skin and make you into a new vessel. Paul tells you the flesh lusts against the Spirit and the Spirit against the flesh. This is the definition of the struggle you will experience mentally and physically. This brings to light what he wrote in Romans 7:14-24. There is no possible way to mix the two and there is no rest both can coexist in.

**Ezekiel 36:26-27, 31** *I will give you a new heart and put a new spirit within you; I will take the heart of stone out of your flesh and give you a heart of flesh. I will put My Spirit within you and cause you to walk in My statutes, and you will keep My judgments and do them.... Then you will remember your evil ways and your deeds that were not good; and you will loathe yourselves in your own sight, for your iniquities and your abominations.*

You read in the old covenant a promise of a new covenant, a new ability to relate with God. Notice this is a gift from your heavenly Father and it is now personal. The work performed is done supernaturally and brings about physical changes in your nature and character that every eye can see (Isaiah 61:9).

Notice the Holy Spirit brings back the remembrance ("remember your evil ways"), not therapy or the various methods of man. He gives you the desire to repent and to seek redemption and forgiveness. He causes a change within your heart so you hunger after God's heart and ways. He gives you balance in your repentance so even though you are sorrowful, you are not overwhelmed or lost in hopelessness. With God, there is balance in sorrow. Whenever He disciplines, He also gives hope for change and the future. Whenever He chastens, scourges, or rebukes, He always gives instructions with love for correction and a life in righteousness and again, a hope for the future. God desires you to be completely clean in His sight so He shows you how to confess your ways, deeds, iniquities, and abominations. He leaves no foothold for the enemy.

Lastly, you are no longer under the law if you are led by or surrendered to the Holy Spirit. Romans 6:14 declares sin has lost its ability to dominate you because of the blood of Jesus Christ which was shed for you on the cross. Now you are born in the Spirit and, therefore, above the law. Whereas before Christ entered your heart, you were under the law and you remained carnal—sold under sin (Romans 7:14). Christ has now purchased you and made you free in Him (1 Corinthians 6:20; Luke 4:18; Isaiah 61:1-3; 2 Corinthians 3:17).

**Romans 8:5-9** *For those who live according to the flesh set their minds on the things of the flesh, but those who live according to the Spirit, the things of the Spirit. For to be carnally minded is death, but to* *be spiritually minded is life and peace. Because the carnal mind is enmity against God; for it is not subject to the law of God, nor indeed can be. So then, those who are in the flesh cannot please God. But you are not in the flesh but in the Spirit, if indeed the Spirit of God dwells in you. Now if anyone does not have the Spirit of Christ, he is not His.*

Here you see the difference between the fleshly mindset and the spiritual mindset. You see the results of having a wrong focus. Focus affects six different items in your life. The first three start with "D" and are <u>direction</u>, <u>desires</u>, and <u>devotion</u>. The second set begins with "W" and are <u>worship</u>, <u>works</u>, and <u>walk</u>. They can all cause a rippling effect on one another, as well as stand independently of each other. When your mind is set on the things of this world and your flesh, you are told of the promise of death. If it is set on the things of heaven and the Spirit—there is life and peace. As was stated earlier in this lesson, your carnal mind is in enmity against God and is irreconcilable. This is positive proof nothing done in the flesh is acceptable to Him nor will it last.

The moment you accept Jesus into your heart you are filled with His Spirit. You cannot be in the flesh if the Holy Spirit dwells within you and you are "born again." This is what the Apostle John (1 John 3:4-9) means when he states a Christian cannot sin. Because of your new nature, you will not practice sin as a way of life. You are now beginning to learn new habits in righteousness. You now hate the sin you do, and when you do commit sin, you repent of it and turn from it. It also points out clearly if you don't turn from your sins and receive conviction from the Holy Spirit about your sin, you are not "born again" and you are not His. For a review, see the section on repentance in Lesson 1.

**1 John 3:18-24** *My little children, let us not love in word or in tongue, but in deed and in truth. 19 And by this we know that we are of the truth, and shall assure our hearts before Him. 20 For if our heart condemns us, God is greater than our heart, and knows all things. 21 Beloved, if our heart does not condemn us, we have confidence toward God. 22 And whatever we ask we receive from Him, because we keep His commandments and do those things that are pleasing in His sight. 23 And this is His commandment: that we should believe on the name of His Son Jesus Christ and love one another, as He gave us commandment. 24 Now he who keeps His commandments abides in Him, and He in him. And by this we know that He abides in us, by the Spirit whom He has given us.*

In these verses you see the proof of your regeneration. You begin to <u>do</u> rather than just speak. You receive assurance because of your actions and your heart is established before God Almighty. You also receive the promises of God because of faith. You need confidence in the everlasting mercy and love your heavenly Father has for you. Remember what **Romans 8:1** says, "*There is therefore now no condemnation to those who are in Christ Jesus, who do not walk according to the flesh, but according to the Spirit.*"

Because of the confidence you are now given and the security that is developed within your heart, you know when (1) God hears your requests, and (2) your requests are in line with His will, (3) because of your obedience, and (4) because of the guidance of the Holy Spirit, you know full well you will have what you ask for.

In verses 23 and 24, you see three things that need to be visible in your life to prove to everyone around you, including yourself, that you are in Christ. These are (1) truly believe on the name of His Son, which coincidentally is the work of God (John 6:29), (2) love one another, and (3) keep His commandments. These show you are truly abiding in Him.

**Abide:** *To remain, abide; in reference to place a. to sojourn, tarry, b. not to depart, c. to continue to be present, d. to be held, kept, continually; in reference to time a. to continue to be, not to perish, to last, endure, b. of persons, to survive, live; in reference to state or condition a. to remain as one, not to become another or different* (OLB).

The final proof of your security is your relationship with the Holy Spirit. He resides within you, never to leave you, nor forsake you. He is your guarantee, your seal, your down payment, and your earnest payment on heaven. Without Him, you would never know sin, be convicted of it, learn to do good, or be able to produce fruits of righteousness. You would never know the freedom of dying to self and having the power to love others <u>as much as</u> you already love yourself. You would never know the joy of serving others. You would never see the need to mourn over the sin of others instead of calling attention to it or sometimes seeking revenge for it. He enables you to exhibit the fruits of the Spirit, which are love, joy, peace, longsuffering, kindness, goodness, faithfulness, gentleness, and self-control.

**Romans 12:1-3** *I beseech you therefore, brethren, by the mercies of God, that you present your bodies a living sacrifice, holy, acceptable to God, which is your reasonable service. And do not be conformed to this world, but be transformed by the renewing of your mind, that you may prove what is that good and acceptable and perfect will of God. For I say, through the grace given to me, to everyone who is among you, not to think of himself more highly than he ought to think, but to think soberly, as God has dealt to each one a measure of faith.*

These verses show the growing confidence you obtain when the will of God is lived out in your heart and life. When you respond to the tender mercies of God, which allow you to present your body as a living sacrifice, you mirror the obedience of Jesus Christ. When this happens, you learn from your suffering the blessing of obedience and obtain its wonderful results. *Therefore if there is any consolation in Christ, if any comfort of love, if any fellowship of the Spirit, if any affection and mercy, fulfill my joy by being like-minded, having the same love, being of one accord, of one mind. Let nothing be done through selfish ambition or conceit, but in lowliness of mind let each esteem others better than himself. Let each of you look out not only for his own interests, but also for the interests of others… Who, in the days of His flesh, when He had offered up prayers and supplications, with vehement cries and tears to Him who was able to save Him from death, and was heard because of His godly fear, though He was a Son, yet He learned obedience by the things which He suffered. And having been perfected, He became the author of eternal salvation to all who obey Him,…*

You are holy, acceptable, and reasonable in your service to God. What has He held back from you? Is it unreasonable to hold back from Him anything He has first given to and for you? Is it out of line to give your all to Him and for Him? With the Spirit working in and through your mind, you now see what is real and true. You are now able to resist the pressures of the world and avoid its molds, philosophies, and principles (Colossians 2:8, 20). You are renewed in your mind, which means your thinking patterns and processes; you are hungry for the will of God instead of your own. The obvious result of this is the ability to put others before you, placing them second in priority of importance, and yourself third. It is the result of grace working in your life. It is the definition of <u>thinking soberly</u>: 1. *to have understanding, be wise,* 2. *to feel, to think,* 2a. *to have an opinion of one's self, think of one's self, to be modest, not let one's opinion (though just) of himself exceed the bounds of modesty,* 2b. *to think or judge what one's opinion is,* 2c. *to be of the same mind, i.e., agreed together, cherish the same views* (OLB).

What kind of peace do you enjoy when your mind lines up with your Creator? This is the result of thinking soberly.

**Romans 13:11-14** *And do this, knowing the time, that now it is high time to awake out of sleep; for now our salvation is nearer than when we first believed. The night is far spent, the day is at hand. Therefore let us cast off the works of darkness, and let us put on the armor of light. Let us walk properly, as in the day, not in revelry and drunkenness, not in lewdness and lust, not in strife and envy. But put on the Lord Jesus Christ, and make no provision for the flesh, to fulfill its lusts.*

These verses demonstrate as you allow the Holy Spirit to search you and know you, you begin to awaken to the glory and light of the work of God within your life. You begin to react to the anticipation of the LORD's return and you eagerly await and call out for its fulfillment. You realize stewardship of time is a gift and realize all the time you have wasted. You go to work and begin to use time to your advantage instead of wasting it. Once again, you are instructed to cast off the old man and his works and put on the armor of light. You are enabled to walk properly. You are, through faith, trust, and obedience, enabled to put away the works of the flesh and able to put on Christ. By doing so, you are able to avoid any provision for the flesh and able to crucify the flesh and all its lusts (*desire, craving, longing, and desire for what is forbidden* (OLB)).

## Introduction to the Inventory

**Psalms 139:23-24** *Search me, O God, and know my heart; try me, and know my anxieties; and see if there is any wicked way in me, and lead me in the way everlasting.*

As you approach the footwork of Principle 4 by doing an inventory (which is the proof of your newfound faith in Christ), you must ask yourself: are you fearful, anxious, or worried about what you might face? This is not only understandable but is an expected reaction of your flesh or sinful nature. The scripture states you hate the light as long as you are in darkness, and you fear the possibility your deeds might be exposed. **John 3:19-20**, *"And this is the condemnation, that the light has come into the world, and men loved darkness rather than light, because their deeds were evil. For everyone practicing evil hates the light and does not come to the light, lest his deeds should be exposed."* You have also been humbled by your past to the point you are now not proud of what you once were, and it now causes you shame, guilt, regret, and remorse. **Romans 6:21**, *"What fruit did you have then in the things of which you are now ashamed? For the end of those things is death."*

Now, as a child of God and believing you have a loving heavenly Father, you must accept His way of bringing you closer to Him despite what your feelings try to tell you. You have learned through the scriptures and the fruit that has been born in your new life in Christ that your feelings or emotions are not a valid or trustworthy compass to the obedience and ways of God. They cannot be trusted in the majority of circumstances. Therefore, you must believe the scriptures when they tell you God loves you and, therefore, He will discipline you. **Hebrews 12:6-7, 11**, *"For whom the LORD loves He chastens, and scourges every son whom He receives. If you endure chastening, God deals with you as with sons; for what son is there whom a father does not chasten?... Now no chastening seems to be joyful for the present, but painful; nevertheless, afterward it yields the peaceable fruit of righteousness to those who have been trained by it."*

**Isaiah 1:16-18** *"Wash yourselves, make yourselves clean; put away the evil of your doings from before My eyes. Cease to do evil, learn to do good; seek justice, rebuke the oppressor; defend the fatherless, plead for the widow. Come now, and let us reason together," says the LORD, "Though your sins are like scarlet, they shall be as white as snow; though they are red like crimson, they shall be as wool."*

We must remember the LORD wants us to reason with Him about our true nature and to learn a whole and fruitful way of life.

God has made everything possible for you to be clean and sober before Him through His grace. He has made provision for every change that is required for your life to be abundant and overflowing. He starts by changing the inside of you.

You need to ask yourself at this point, why would God, after doing all these good things in you and for you, want you to remember (look at) your "evil ways and deeds" and to loathe yourself for your "iniquities and abominations"? (Ezekiel 36:26-27, 31) In **Psalms 36:1-2** you are told, *"An oracle within my heart concerning the transgression of the wicked: there is no fear of God before his eyes. For he flatters himself in his own eyes, when he finds out his iniquity and when he hates."*

If you state you are without sin, you deceive yourself and, furthermore, the truth is not in you! In essence, God is telling you He associates your refusal to identify sin with a love for wickedness. When you deceive yourself by refusing to identify these things in your life, it shows your understanding of your relationship with God and His Word is hindered and may not have a place in you. (Ephesians 1:6; 1 John 1:8-10)

**John 15:1-2** *I am the true vine, and My Father is the vinedresser. Every branch in Me that does not bear fruit He takes away; and every branch that bears fruit He prunes, that it may bear more fruit.*

If you truly believe God's Word that this process is biblical and a necessity for you to be clean and sober, you are now obediently ready to begin. Since confess means to acknowledge, you can begin by asking the Holy Spirit to guide you in identifying to what extent the strengths and weaknesses (personality traits) in your life manifest themselves. It also shows the full extent and truth of your repentance as you do everything possible to have your life restored by Christ. Read 2 Corinthians 7:10-11.

**1 Thessalonians 5:23-24** *Now may the God of peace Himself sanctify you completely; and may your whole spirit, soul, and body be preserved blameless at the coming of our Lord Jesus Christ. He who calls you is faithful, who also will do it.*

You will get some idea of this cleansing as you check the appropriate columns in the following inventory. Be sure of the following promises as you begin this process (Philippians 1:6; Hebrews 13:20-21).

# Principle 4 Inventory

A = Very little (practically never)
B = Occasionally (some of the time)
C = Considerably (most of the time)
D = Consistently (almost always)

| Fruitlessness | A | B | C | D |
| --- | --- | --- | --- | --- |

_____

1. Self-Pity
2. Resentful
3. Critical
4. Suspicious
5. Angry
6. Tense and apprehensive
7. Emotionally uncontrolled
8. Withdrawn
9. Jealous
10. Fearful (afraid to assert self)
11. Selfish, self-indulgent
12. Domineering
13. Self-righteous
14. Stubborn
15. Intolerant
16. Dishonest with self
17. Sexual fantasizing
18. Depressed and gloomy
19. Smug, narrow-minded
20. Feeling superior
21. Expect too much too soon
22. Hyper-sensitive
23. Despondent
24. Sullen (silent treatment)
25. Apprehensive of the future
26. Procrastinating
27. Aimless and indifferent

| Fruitfulness | A | B | C | D |
| --- | --- | --- | --- | --- |

_____

1. Unselfish, thoughtful of others
2. Not holding grudges
3. Charitable
4. Trusting
5. Patient
6. Relaxed
7. Calm
8. Outgoing
9. Loving in attitude
10. Confident
11. Generous and loving
12. Yielding
13. Uncritical
14. Agreeable
15. Forgiving
16. Truthful
17. Meditation of God's Word
18. Optimistic and cheerful
19. Open-minded, gracious
20. Humble
21. Realistic
22. Willing to admit faults
23. Hopeful
24. Having a sense of humor
25. Living 24 hours a day
26. Being prompt
27. Finding a purpose

28. Excessive television

29. Worrisome, over-anxious

30. Ungrateful

31. Prone to gossip

32. Obsessed with own problems

28. Spiritual reading (studying)

29. Serene

30. Thankful for all blessings

31. Protect confidences of others

32. Helpful to others

**Note:** Retain this form in your records. Periodically you will have the opportunity to do it again and when you do, you will be blessed by the progress you will have made.

# Conclusion

REMEMBER, God tells you in **Romans 8:1**, *"There is therefore now no condemnation to those who are in Christ Jesus, who do not walk according to the flesh, but according to the Spirit."* Because you now can hear and are able to follow the Holy Spirit's directions, you are committed to allow Him to guide you and reveal to you the current condition of your strengths, weaknesses, and character. You are now ready to proceed to Principle 5.

## Questions for Lesson 3

1. Why would you accurately call this a God search instead of a personal inventory? What is the reason your conscience would now want to be clean and pure before God?

2. What is the boundary, periphery, or border of liberty, freedom, or grace? What are your two choices for your focus?

3. What are the three D's and three W's?

4. What are the four reasons you can have confidence in God to answer your requests?

5. What is the manifested evidence that shows you are truly abiding in Christ?

6. What is the definition of thinking soberly?

7. What is the definition of lusts?

8. What does confess mean and how do you confess your sins to God, on your own or with the Holy Spirit's help?

# Rid of Shame and Guilt

I started going to Pure Word in 1998 when I was in my second year of a three-year prison sentence. A woman I had met in jail five years before was going to lead it and I thought I would go and check it out. I saw what God was doing in her life and said "Wow! I want that!" I surrendered my life to the Lord but didn't really give it all up to Him. I didn't understand yet about grace and His full love for me. I thought God did forgive me but I thought I had this awful disease of drug addiction that I would have to work to keep at bay and that my kids would also have it. I carried that shame and guilt not knowing God would take all that, too.

Boy, were my eyes opened when I learned through God, the Bible, and Pure Word about God's healing—saving—forgiving—loving grace; I didn't have to work steps or remember all the old bad stuff I had done over and over again to stay sober. Jesus carried all that for me. All I had to do was surrender to Him all of it—and I mean all of it. But that wasn't easy for me because in my head it was too easy. Going to the Pure Word meetings I learned just how to do it. The Lord used the women who lead the Pure Word group at the Women's Correctional Work Center. Boy did they have their hands full with me. I would ask so many questions sometimes they didn't get to do their whole lesson. They would look to God's Word for the answers. That was great. Sometimes I was afraid they wouldn't come back as much as I bugged them. But they did every week and all of us looked forward to seeing them.

I got out in March of 1999 and never looked back—only forward to the Lord. I continue to go to Pure Word because I still have many questions I ask Pastor Randy. The Lord has so blessed my life through Pure Word. (Not that I don't have struggles. But when I do I have God and my Pure Word family to help me through them and it is so much easier than trying to do it on my own.)

I now am doing great in the Lord and I even do a Pure Word Bible study in my home on Monday nights. I plan on going back into the prison to do Pure Word when my children get older.

Linda

# Lesson 4: The Importance of Forgiveness, Principles 5-7

The principles you now will survey are probably the key points to the progression of your growth in Christ and the maturing process of sobriety. These principles place the faith that has developed within your heart, whether great or small, in the spotlight for all to see.

Because of the completion of the first four principles, there is a newly-developed desire to obey the will of God. Your zeal for this new life has manifested within you as a result of having received this gift from your heavenly Father by grace through faith. It has begun to bubble to the top of you and is now running over. You now have a deeper understanding of the love God has for you, as well as a stronger desire for the freedom that results from your obedience to His Word. You now see through the eyes of your heart the hope, faith, and promises that are stated in God's Word and these principles. As a result of the fulfilled promises and the manifestation of fruit that has been born into your life, you now trust in Him and endeavor to complete the remaining principles that follow.

The next three principles deal with the foundation and truth that the forgiveness of God causes to manifest within you as you grow, mature, and practice the God-directed changes in your life. They deal mainly with the area of forgiveness and the beginning process of the desire to reconcile. There is so much misinformation dispersed about forgiveness that you need to begin with a basic foundation.

You are inculcated or trained into believing you must forgive yourself in order to experience fulfillment, peace, happiness, and joy. How many of you have heard or believed this? How many of you have stated to yourself or to others, "Even though I know God has forgiven me, I just can't forgive myself for what I have done." Maybe you've heard from well-meaning people, even Christians in the ministry, "You must forgive yourself to get rid of this guilt, shame, and condemnation." Even you, as a child of God, might erroneously say, "Now that God has forgiven me I must strive to learn how to forgive myself." Feelings of guilt, shame, and condemnation indicate you still need to rest your hope on the promises of God concerning what He says in His Word about His forgiveness of your sins. Read Psalms 103:12; Romans 5:1-2; Colossians 1:21-23; and Hebrews 11:6.

The problem with this sophistry (a deceptive or misleading method of reasoning) is that it causes you to exalt yourself. This kind of thinking causes you to elevate your own works, thoughts, and desires (lusts) above the finished work of Christ on the cross. You, as a child of God, must rest on the promises and provision of His forgiveness. God's Word states clearly there is no condemnation in Him <u>regardless</u> of your feelings, circumstances, or understanding (1 John 3:20). To believe anything else is to say to Him that His perfect work is not sufficient and it is somehow incomplete. God does all the work, and there is nothing you can do to add to it or take away from it. In Him alone are you made complete. See 1 John 1:9; Romans 8:1; Philippians 1:6; 2:13; Colossians 2:10; 1 Thessalonians 5:24; 1 John 2:5; and John 15:5.

To forgive is to trust God in all things. Unforgiveness shows you don't trust Him to be your protector and provider. The truth of the matter is trust <u>will not manifest</u> until there is complete forgiveness in the heart of the individual who is seeking to forgive.

Trust is the second reaction caused by forgiveness, not the first, as is often sought after when you are in the flesh. Remember, forgiveness came first from God and then you began to trust Him for it (1 John 4:10, 19; Romans 5:6, 8). Recognize forgiveness <u>is a choice</u>, not a feeling. Your feelings <u>will change</u> when you <u>exercise obedience</u> to God's commands. You are commanded to forgive; it is not an option.

Forgiveness was given by your heavenly Father before you ever knew you needed it. Now that you have it, you are to give it away as abundantly as it has been provided to you. Remember, forgiveness is totally undeserved and cannot be earned. If you are normal, you won't ever feel like forgiving when you are sinned against. You want to stew on the wrong done to you, you want revenge, and if not dealt with by the blood of Jesus, you become bitter, resentful, and angry. All sin, no matter the size, leaves you with a bitter taste that is impossible to get rid of without the help of God.

Remember this nonnegotiable and important fact. If you consistently refuse to forgive as you are instructed to do in the scriptures, it indicates the work of regeneration has not been completed or <u>possibly</u>, not even started (1 John 2:3-4, 9-11; 3:6, 9-10, 15; 4:20-21). It shows you are still controlled by the flesh and not the Spirit of God. If you still have a desire for revenge and your focus is on yourself instead of God and others, it shows your heart still does not recognize nor understand the totality of your forgiveness (Matthew 18:23-35; Luke 7:47).

If this is the case, you need to be honest with yourself. Revisit the last two principles and allow the good, acceptable, and perfect will of God to take place within your heart so the necessary fruits of forgiveness and mercy can take place. With this stated and fresh in the forefront of your mind, let's look now at the next principle in this series.

**Principle 5 - *AFTER RECOGNIZING THE EXACT NATURE, CAUSE, AND RESPONSIBILITY FOR MY SIN, I'M NOW READY FOR THE NEXT STEP TOWARD FREEDOM IN CHRIST. I NOW RECOGNIZE THE NEED FOR ACCOUNTABILITY IN ORDER TO HELP ME MAINTAIN A TRUTHFUL AND OPEN WALK WITH JESUS AND MAN. THEREFORE, I'M WILLING TO CONFESS MY SINS TO GOD AND ANOTHER PERSON, AND IN DOING SO, I SOLIDIFY THE TRUTH OF MY SIN FOR THE FIRST TIME.***

This principle is the first in the series you must take in order truly to experience the freedom available to you in Christ. When you confess your sins to God and someone else, you begin to initiate the process that will result in your no longer carrying the condemnation, guilt, and shame that has burdened you throughout your lifetime of addiction (Psalms 32:3).

Principle 5 is also a beginning for healing. See Psalms 32:5-7. As you begin to confess these hidden sins, the LORD will begin to heal you of maladies like ulcers, tumors, depression, double-mindedness, or illnesses. These afflicted you because of your ignorance or inner conflict that went on inside of you because of unconfessed sin (Ezekiel 36:31-35, James 5:16). Remember, sin is defined three ways by the scriptures.

**Transgressions**: *Rebellion, sin, trespass* (OLB). These are sins we knowingly commit.

**Iniquity**: To commit sin without knowledge, to commit sin intrinsically, perversity, depravity. *1. to bend, twist, distort, to do perversely, to be bent, be bowed down, be twisted, be perverted, 2. to commit iniquity, do wrong, pervert* (OLB).

**Sin**: *Miss, miss the way, go wrong, incur guilt, to miss the goal or mark, to miss the path of right and duty, to incur guilt, incur penalty by sin, and to forfeit* (OLB).

**Psalms 32:1-5** *Blessed is he whose transgression is forgiven, whose sin is covered. 2 Blessed is the man to whom the LORD does not impute iniquity, and in whose spirit there is no deceit. 3 When I kept silent, my bones grew old through my groaning all the day long. 4 For day and night Your hand was heavy upon me; my vitality was turned into the drought of summer. 5 I acknowledged my sin to You, and my iniquity I have not hidden. I said, "I will confess my transgressions to the LORD," and You forgave the iniquity of my sin.*

The first two verses of this Psalm present a very contrite and broken King David. He begins with a foundational truth—the blessings of having all your sins forgiven. David points to a source outside of himself that grants this forgiveness. He doesn't say—*blessed is the man who forgives himself of all his own transgression and sin, who doesn't impute to himself all of his iniquities and in whom there resides a spirit that has no guile.* No, he states there is a power that is greater than himself that needs to do this cleaning, and only God can clean his conscience to the point that his soul can rest.

Verse 3 of Psalm 32 points out the truth of the consequences you reap when you don't follow the direction and will of God. David gives a vivid picture of the results of unconfessed sin in a life. He states his bones grew old (a word picture); you can feel very old when your conscience is weighed down. Although the effects are immediate in your spirit, your sins can manifest in the soul and cause physical effects to afflict your body. Here's a sample list: adultery, anxiety, outbursts of anger or temper tantrums, anorexia, arrogance, bitterness, bulimia, ineffective or evil communications, depression, lack of discipline, drunkenness, fear, financial problems, fornication, frustration, gluttony, greed, guilt, homosexuality, impatience, interpersonal disputes, jealousy, laziness, loneliness, lust, lying, marriage problems and failures, problems in parent and child relationships, pride, procrastination, rebellion, self-pity, stealing, suffering, ulcers, and worry—virtually every area of life. Some of these sins are very debilitating and can, at times, if not repented of and forsaken, cause death. Remember, ignorance—neither an excuse nor covering for sin—is fixable. Stupidity though, is a choice.

Verse 4 continues to show you the consequences of not confessing sins to your loving heavenly Father. It saps your strength and your resources. Unconfessed sins dry you up in spirit, soul, and body.

Verse 5 shows the results of turning to a merciful God and how He died to show you how serious He was to love you and forgive you completely. David again stresses the importance of having all your sin, transgression, and iniquity forgiven. He doesn't leave any chances for darkness to grow in him and stand between himself and God.

Also, note the use of David's will. He states emphatically, *"I acknowledged my sin to You, and my iniquity I have not hidden,"* and *"I will confess my transgressions to the LORD."*

**LORD:**   *The proper name of the one true God* (OLB). This title is spoken in place of Yahweh in Jewish display of reverence, firm, strong, master, king, Lord of the whole earth, Adonai (parallel with Yahweh).

King David knew whom he had sinned against. He fully understood the only One who could give complete forgiveness for all he had done. Here you see the value of both confession and acknowledgment to a Holy God. <u>Acknowledge</u> means t*o know, learn to know (become sensitive to), to perceive and see, find out and discern, to discriminate, distinguish; to know by experience; to recognize, admit, acknowledge, confess; to conside*r (OLB). <u>Confess</u> means to identify, agree, accept, and understand what you have done. You need to acknowledge your sin and then confess it, just as David did.

**Proverbs 28:13** *He who covers his sins will not prosper, but whoever confesses and forsakes them will have mercy.*

In this verse you have a promise some might not consider positive, but it is. It promises mercy to those who know the LORD as Savior and King because sin is like cancer. Cancer, if left to prosper by itself, just like sin, will eventually kill. If you are a child of the King, you will not prosper in your sin nor will you be able to cover it up. God, in His mercy, will reveal it.

The word prosper is not limited to finances as you might first think; it also covers the health, emotional, legal, and spiritual areas. You will see deterioration in every major life area when you sin, slow at first because of God's mercy, but with increasing velocity. God is slow to act, and sometimes you mistake His mercy and longsuffering for the misconceived idea you have somehow escaped His sight.

**Ecclesiastes 8:11** *Because the sentence against an evil work is not executed speedily, therefore the heart of the sons of men is fully set in them to do evil.*

**Jeremiah 2:19** *"Your own wickedness will correct you, and your backslidings will rebuke you. Know therefore and see that it is an evil and bitter thing that you have forsaken the LORD your God, and the fear of Me is not in you," says the Lord GOD of hosts.*

You must remember either your sin will correct you or it will be exposed. God allows this because you are His child, and He only disciplines those whom He loves. If you do not receive God's discipline, then you are not His. The LORD loves you and will use everything in His power to save you, discipline you, correct you, and train you in righteousness. He chastens and scourges you because of His mercy, compassion, and love for you (Numbers 32:23; Hebrews 12:5-11). He knows better than you that <u>SIN KILLS</u>!

**Luke 12:2-3** *For there is nothing covered that will not be revealed, nor hidden that will not be known. Therefore whatever you have spoken in the dark will be heard in the light, and what you have spoken in the ear in inner rooms will be proclaimed on the housetops.*

The LORD tells you what your consequences will be if you try to prosper in the ways of evil. When you are in self-deception, you believe the LORD doesn't see. You are truly mistaken.

**Ezekiel 8:12** *Then He said to me, "Son of man, have you seen what the elders of the house of Israel do in the dark, every man in the room of his idols? For they say, `The LORD does not see us, the LORD has forsaken the land.'"*

The LORD sees all you do. He will reward both the good, as well as the bad. He has no favorites; He knows and loves His own (1 John 2:1-2, 2 Corinthians 5:10).

**Philippians 3:13** *Brethren, I do not count myself to have apprehended; but one thing I do, forgetting those things which are behind and reaching forward to those things which are ahead...*

One of the liberating results of following through and exercising obedience to the Word of God is the ability to learn from and look at the course of events that have transpired in your past <u>without</u> condemnation. You are humble in heart; the result of the new character developing within you is the ability not to take yourself so seriously. Although you take your mistakes seriously, you can now look at them in the light of God's grace and mercy, knowing His love covers a multitude of sins. You are now able to think logically about your mistakes and discern why you made them without fear and anxious desires. You are now enabled to control the temptation to run. You can now think through your options by yourself or, if possible, with a discipler. You begin to desire to learn and be taught in this new way of living. The result is a zeal with a desire to be responsible and accountable.

**James 5:16** *Confess your trespasses to one another, and pray for one another, that you may be healed. The effective, fervent prayer of a righteous man avails much.*

In this verse, you have an illustration of the necessary heart condition and the actions the individual needs to take to heal. Notice the individual has to take an action before any healing can take place.

It is much like the story of the man with the withered hand (Mark 3:1-6; Luke 6:6-11). He had to stretch it out before it could be healed. The faith of the man had to be exercised and appropriated before the healing could take place. He first had to overcome what he felt or saw, and second, he had to believe Jesus was greater than the current set of circumstances he found himself in.

This individual needs to cry out to God and agree with God that he has transgressed. Then he needs to confess to another individual he has sinned. He needs to pray with them, pray for them, and thank God he has them in his life. He needs to ask God for his healing and believe he will receive it.

Lastly, he needs to believe the prayer offered up in faith will bring about the desired healing being requested and the prayers of the righteous will bring about great results. These prayers are not to be a one-time event but are to be frequent and consistent. They are to be offered up with the heart, the mind-set, and attitude which are described in Matthew 7:7-8. You are to believe God hears you, and you are to ask according to His will. When you do, you will have what you petition. You have His Word on it (1 John 5:14-15).

There is an undiscovered blessing of doing and completing this principle. It is a fact you now will have confidants who love and care for you in a way you have never had nor experienced before. They will bring the Word of God to you in a way that will bring healing for your heart and soul. They will encourage and uplift you in such a way as to cause you to aspire to new heights in faith which you couldn't have ever imagined. They will encourage, rebuke, correct, and train you in the ways of the

LORD. You will, in turn, desire to learn this new way of living and will respond to them, as well as the LORD, with obedience. You will build confidence in their counsel and will learn to compare what counsel is given with the Word of God. You will grow in the habit of using the Word and in your dependence upon it for everyday situations and circumstances. You will learn to take in, as well as to give away. You will learn to grow in the area of being served, as well as the importance of serving others. You will become a vessel and a source for living water to be poured out of, as well as knowing where the source of living water comes from. You will have a joyful mouth and an obedient ear. You will be able to answer in season, as well as out of season. You will have confidence and boldness in the counsel you give. (Proverbs 15:23; Proverbs 25:11-12)

**Principle 6 -** *I BECOME ENTIRELY READY AND WILLING TO HAVE GOD BEGIN THE PROCESS OF REMOVING ALL OF THE HABITUAL SINS IN MY LIFE. I REALIZE THIS PROCESS WILL SOMETIMES BE PAINFUL AND TRYING, BUT WITH HIS HELP AND HIS WILL WORKING IN ME TO CONFORM ME TO HIS IMAGE, I KNOW WITH FULL CONFIDENCE HE WILL COMPLETE THIS WORK FULLY.*

By the time you reach Principle 6, your heart has been sensitized to your sin and a true desire to be holy has developed. This is because of God's glorious work and faithfulness to His Word. Your conscience is beginning to be healed from being beaten down or nearly cut off because of your lifestyle of lies and hypocrisy (1 Timothy 4:1-2, Hebrews 9:14). There will also be a certain amount of fruit evident and a willingness and zeal apparent in your life at this point.

You have made this decision and commitment to turn from the things of your past. This includes the memories and old ideas that caused you to stumble (2 Corinthians 10:4-5) and the philosophies of the world that have clouded the truth of God's Word. The fruit that is evident is shown by your faithfulness to follow through with the footwork of allowing God to search you and try your ways. It is also evident by your confession to another person whom God has blessed you with by putting this person in your life to stand beside you and disciple you. You see the ever-fervent love God has for you by His continued discipline, faithfulness, and commitment to show you a new way of life. Ezekiel 36:27 is certainly true because His Spirit is causing you to love and follow His decrees (Psalms 119:15-18, 47-48, 57, 63, 67, 71, 92, 103-104, 133, 140, 142, 161-163, 165).

As you see the results that come from being obedient to do the preceding principles, you are now ready to proceed on to the next with a heart full of hope and joy.

**Hebrews 8:10-12** *For this is the covenant that I will make with the house of Israel after those days, says the LORD: I will put My laws in their mind and write them on their hearts; and I will be their God, and they shall be My people. None of them shall teach his neighbor, and none his brother, saying, `Know the LORD,' for all shall know Me, from the least of them to the greatest of them. For I will be merciful to their unrighteousness, and their sins and their lawless deeds I will remember no more.*

As you read this passage in the scripture, you see the promise of the change of relationship concerning the law. In the Old Covenant, the law was written on tablets of stone and could not reside within you. It was cold, lifeless, and unmerciful and had to be followed to the letter. It required complete perfection. It couldn't regenerate, and it could not translate life.

However, with the New Covenant came a new way to relate to God, which came through the shed blood of your Savior (Luke 22:20). As Jesus stated, He fulfilled the law (Matthew 5:17). Because of this great and perfect work, you now stand before your Father and LORD redeemed and sanctified (Romans 10:4; Galatians 3:24; 4:4-5). Now the Holy Spirit resides within you and you are His temple or tabernacle. You no longer rely on the teaching of men to instruct you through the Word of God because now you have the LORD teaching you (1 John 2:27). Now you are instructed to fellowship and compare all teaching with the Word of God and allow the LORD to correct (Hebrews 10:22-25; Acts 17:11; Philippians 3:15-16; 1 Corinthians 11:19).

This set of scriptures closes with the promise that God will no longer hold you accountable to pay the debt of sin you incurred because of your sins. Jesus has paved the way for mercy and has paid the debt in full.

**Ephesians 1:7** *In Him we have redemption through His blood, the forgiveness of sins, according to the riches of His grace...*

God has done it all for you. Is there any reason why you would think you have to do anything other than believe? See Colossian 2:6. This verse truly spells out grace for you. You have redemption through His blood, the forgiveness of sins, and the riches in His grace.

**Redemption:** *A releasing or liberation effected by payment of ransom or deliverance* (OLB). *It was a price paid for redeeming slaves or captives. It means you were once separated by your sins and incapable of coming together or making peace between you and God. It was the ransom paid for a life. It was paid by Jesus to liberate all who would believe in Him, liberate them from misery and the penalty of their sins.*

**Forgiveness:** *Forgiveness or pardon, of sins (letting them go as if they had never been committed), remission of the penalty; to send away; to let go, let alone, let be; to let go, give up a debt, forgive, to remit; to give up, keep no longer* (OLB).

**Grace:** *Good will, loving-kindness, favor, of the merciful kindness by which God, exerting his holy influence upon souls, turns them to Christ, keeps, strengthens, increases them in Christian faith, knowledge, affection, and kindles them to the exercise of the Christian virtues* (OLB).

**1 Peter 2:24** *...who Himself bore our sins in His own body on the tree, that we, having died to sins, might live for righteousness—by whose stripes you were healed.*

You see what your true healing was and where it took place. It was healing for your soul, not your physical nature. He bore your <u>sins</u> in His own body on the cross. Your healing made way for your ability to obey and be conformed to His image. It broke the chains of rebellion and stubbornness and made way for humbleness and brokenness.

**Hebrews 4:13-16** *And there is no creature hidden from His sight, but all things are naked and open to the eyes of Him to whom we must give account. Seeing then that we have a great High Priest who has passed through the heavens, Jesus the Son of God, let us hold fast our confession. For we do not have a High Priest who cannot sympathize with our weaknesses, but was in all points tempted as we are, yet without* *sin. Let us therefore come boldly to the throne of grace, that we may obtain mercy and find grace to help in time of need.*

Here is the reason you need to become entirely ready and willing to have God remove all your habitual sins. You read that all things are naked and open before His eyes. All will give an account before Him, and none will escape this moment. You know it is impossible for God to forget, and there must be a reckoning of all accounts, whether good or bad. You see Jesus is your great High Priest, and He has gone up through the heavens. He became your point man or trailblazer, as it were, so you could have passage to His Father. You need to hold fast your confession; you need to rest being assured and confident of what He has done. You will tell others of this by your life and words.

Also note Jesus was tempted just as you are in every way. This doesn't mean in every circumstance but that all sin has a root, type, or scheme. These are found in **1 John 2:15-16**, *"Do not love the world or the things in the world. If anyone loves the world, the love of the Father is not in him. For all that is in the world—the lust of the flesh, the lust of the eyes, and the pride of life—is not of the Father but is of the world."* Satan used these same tactics during the temptations against the LORD.

The wonderful truth is you can come to the throne of grace anytime you need to because of your relationship. Notice what you get when you do—mercy and grace in your time of need. Mercy and grace are limitless, and they are usually the first two things you resist the most when you are in the flesh.

**Principle 7 - *I HUMBLY ASK JESUS TO HELP ME TO RECOGNIZE AND REPENT FROM THESE FLAWS IN MY CHARACTER AND BECOME MORE SENSITIVE TO THESE AREAS OF SIN IN MY LIFE I HAVE BEEN HELD CAPTIVE TO (JOHN 8:34). I ALSO ASK HIM TO HELP ME TO LEARN A LIFE OF OBEDIENCE, RATHER THAN A FEELING- OR DESIRE-ORIENTED LIFE AND RECEIVE HIS FORGIVENESS FOR LEADING SUCH A LIFE.***

In Principle 3, you made the <u>decision</u> to turn from the things of the past. Now, by faith you have come to the point in Principle 7 where this decision becomes a reality. **James 4:10** states, *"Humble yourselves in the sight of the Lord, and He will lift you up."* There will be times you will experience the temptation to believe God is not granting your request for deliverance from your sin or sins. There are numerous reasons for this but one may be you have not fully given this issue over to God, or simply put, you are impatient for something to be resolved. You cannot ask God for deliverance from a sin and then keep committing it at the same time. If you ask God for help, you must believe He will help you. You must humble yourself and <u>turn completely away</u> from your sin, whatever it is. You must then <u>learn to recognize these temptations</u> and turn immediately to the LORD for help from <u>His provided resources</u> and strength to resist.

The death of Jesus Christ on the cross has paid the price for all your sins. Now you have the opportunity for forgiveness to become a reality. You need to receive this forgiveness in the areas God revealed to you during the time and process of Principles 4 through 6.

**Psalm 41:4** *I said, "LORD, be merciful to me; heal my soul, for I have sinned against You."*

This passage tells you a truth you don't often think of when you sin. When you sin, you sin against God alone. You at times sin against your brothers or fellow man, but in principle, you sin against God. Jesus stated the greatest commandment was to love God and love your neighbor as much as you already love yourself. When you don't love your neighbor in this manner, you have already broken the first commandment. Therefore, all have sinned against God and Him alone. Also, note David tells you God is perfectly just and blameless when He judges. (Psalm 51:4)

**Luke 18:10-14** *Two men went up to the temple to pray, one a Pharisee and the other a tax collector. The Pharisee stood and prayed thus with himself, `God, I thank You that I am not like other men—extortioners, unjust, adulterers, or even as this tax collector. I fast twice a week; I give tithes of all that I possess.' And the tax collector, standing afar off, would not so much as raise his eyes to heaven, but beat his breast, saying, `God, be merciful to me a sinner!' I tell you, this man went down to his house justified rather than the other; for everyone who exalts himself will be humbled, and he who humbles himself will be exalted.*

This passage shows you the power of self-deception, as well as the power of humility. You see both are despised by the Jews. One, you are told, prays to himself (the Pharisee), the other (the tax collector) prays to God and asks for mercy.

This passage also shows what happens when you have a god of your own understanding. You are not able to discern the true nature or depth of pride or sin. It shuts off your communication with God (Job 35:12; Psalm 66:18; Proverbs 11:2; 16:18; 29:23; Ecclesiastes 7:8; 1 Peter 3:7b). The Pharisee prayed only to himself but thought his prayers were reaching God. He thought his works of religiosity, his position in the public eye, and his place of stature were good enough to pay the price of his sins. He thought a tithe of his heart was all that was required. God requires all that you are and all that you have. When your heart is opened spiritually, you see clearly God owned everything before you even existed. What's even more remarkable is the fact once you give Him everything, He gives it back and more.

The tax collector, on the other hand, came with a broken and contrite heart. He was visibly humbled and poor in Spirit. He would not raise his eyes to heaven because he knew he was not worthy even to speak to such a Holy God. Notice he beat his breast, which is symbolic of the mourning and the grieving for the sins he had committed. His heart hurt, but he could do nothing to ease his pain so he hit himself in the breast to change his focus.

Jesus closes this parable by telling you pride kills and descends, while humility heals and exalts. One causes damnation, while the other causes exaltation.

**1 Peter 5:6-7** *Therefore humble yourselves under the mighty hand of God, that He may exalt you in due time, casting all your care upon Him, for He cares for you.*

This scripture also shows you the value of a humble heart. In order to humble yourself under the mighty hand of God, you must be willing to exalt Him above yourself. Pride causes the disillusioned thought that somehow you are above God in knowledge, wisdom, and understanding. It can even cause you to think you are greater than Him because of the lies spoken to you by the enemy. (Isaiah 14:13-14; 40:13-14; 1 Corinthians 2:16)

# Conclusion

**Hebrews 11:6** *But without faith it is impossible to please Him, for he who comes to God must believe that He is, and that He is a rewarder of those who diligently seek Him.*

You will be rewarded for just believing in the Almighty. You cannot allow your faith to grow stale or stagnant. It is impossible to please Him without faith. So once again you see why you cannot have a god of your own understanding—if you do, then you are not using faith. Faith is the substance of things hoped for, the evidence of things not seen. It isn't something you can come up with on your own, and faith of your own understanding is not pleasing God, but self. Remember this—faith is like calories, you can't see them while you eat them, but you can definitely see their results.

The last three principles develop the middle part of your foundation for your walk in Christ. These principles are not just limited to people with life-controlling problems, they are for anyone who desires a closer walk with the LORD.

The awesome thing about these truths is that anyone who comes to the LORD with these attributes within him will complete these principles, whether he is by grace trying to recover and be redeemed in his life or just trying to draw closer to the LORD because he loves Him. The power of His Word and the healing truths within its pages promises every individual who diligently seeks after Him will find Him, and He will heal him. You have His Word on it! (Job 5:17-18; Proverbs 8:17; Isaiah 57:18-19; Jeremiah 17:14, 29:13)

<u>**Remember - I can "Trust" GOD!!**</u>
<u>**By trusting Him, I show the reality of my faith.**</u>

# Questions for Lesson 4

1. Why are statements such as these untrue?

*"Even though I know God has forgiven me, I just can't forgive myself for what I have done."*
*"You must forgive yourself to get rid of this guilt, shame, and condemnation."*
*"Now that God has forgiven me, I must strive to learn how to forgive myself."*

2. What is a sophistry?

3. What is the definition of sin?

4. What does acknowledge and confess mean?

5. What happens to your sin and you when you have a god of your own understanding?

6. Why is faith so important and why can't faith be in your own understanding?

# Removing my Fears

I began using when I was a young woman—crack cocaine was my drug of choice. I was addicted for eight years and my whole life was a mess. I knew God was calling me but I refused to hear His voice. At one point, I felt someone was going to kill me, I was going to kill someone, or I was simply going to die. My struggle with drugs did not end there; I continued to use other drugs and believed I was OK because I wasn't using cocaine. I was wrong. As my life continued to spin out of control, I was again addicted to Xanex. My daughter, who was 8, kept telling me, "Mom, you need Jesus." I didn't think I needed anyone. Nobody could help me and they certainly did not know my heart and I wasn't going to tell them. At the end of this chapter of my life was Jesus.

I was in Reno with my third husband who had thrown my daughter and me out of his father's house. I was driving around crying and not knowing where to turn as I did not want to call on my family again after many years of failures and desperate phone calls. Eventually, my daughter and I ended up at a motel in Fernley, NV. I did call someone, my sister and her husband. They, once again, came to my rescue. It was at that time I met Jesus. They prayed for my little girl and me. We both accepted Jesus into our hearts. For the first time in three years, I slept without the help of a drug. I was lost but now I'm found, was blind but now I see. All I needed was Jesus.

I prayed and listened to pastors on the radio for the six-hour drive home and knew my life had changed. I had lived in fear, self-centeredness, and sin. Now, I had a new life and hope. There was a peace within me I had never found until I found Jesus. I began to read my Bible and pray. Jesus had opened my eyes to the truth and I couldn't get enough. I hungered and thirsted for His word and righteousness.

The verse that first came to me was Philippians 4:6-7, "Be anxious for nothing, but in everything by prayer and supplication with thanksgiving, let your requests be made known to God and the peace of God which surpasses all understanding will guard your hearts and minds through Christ Jesus." He removed and continues to remove my fears and gives me peace in my heart and mind.

Jesus continues to mold me day by day. As Philippians 1:6 says I can be "confident of this very thing, that He who has begun a good work in you will complete it until the day of Jesus Christ." My hope is in Him. It's His work in me that has changed my life.

There are many struggles and trials in my life as a Christian but I can't imagine facing them without Jesus. 1 Peter 5:6-7 says, "Therefore humble yourselves under the mighty hand of God, that He may exalt you in due time, casting all your cares upon Him, for He cares for you." 1 Corinthians 1:10 says Jesus "who delivered us from so great a death and does deliver us; in whom we trust that He will still deliver us."

I continue to tell myself daily—it's not about me, it's about Jesus. His promises are true and I pray daily for more faith to trust Him and walk in His ways. I know He will never leave me or forsake me as He promises in Hebrews 13:5. I don't know what my future holds but I do know it is in God's hands and there I rest and find peace.

Rhonda

# Lesson 5: The Fruit of Forgiveness, Principles 8-9

In this principle, you come to the bridge that covers the gap of unbelief and intellectual assent. On one side of the gap, you have faith and belief, and on the other side, you have unbelief and doubt. Here you are allowed to see the manifested works of faith. Faith is a verb. It causes you to take actions that you, on your own volition, would not be able to convince yourself to do. You lack the courage and are held back in fear. Faith takes place within a heart where only God can see. He causes your works from faith to be observed on the outside from the belief that has begun to grow on the inside. The actions that take place now will let everyone see the supernatural work of the LORD being done through faith within your heart. Faith manifests through the desires for peace and reconciliation. Your conscience has once again been made sensitive and responsive because of the love God has birthed within your heart. You now are willing to try to make amends wherever possible. A desire for reconciliation is the natural result of the fruit of forgiveness.

To reconcile is to have God bring healing and peace between two souls. God's method of producing reconciliation goes beyond our reason, emotions, or inclination. True reconciliation can only be imparted by God and the recognized need for this gift can only be imputed by God into the heart of man. Man, on his own, never feels like forgiving, let alone reconciling. Examples of reconciliation in scriptures are: God to man (2 Cor 5:18-6:2; Col 1:20); Jacob and Esau (Gen 33); and Joseph and his brothers (Gen 45).

You must keep in mind there will be times when you will be prevented from making clean and clear reconciliation. These are times you must be open to the LORD to do His wonderful work of healing and remain willing to be obedient at a moment's notice. These are the times when your faith will be seen as trust. There also will be times reconciliation will not take place but that is not ours to judge. The timing upon which this process takes place and the length of the season with which it takes to complete it is totally up to God. Your heart, in the meantime, must remain open to the possibilities of reconciliation, as well as the possibility of not being able to reconcile, and you must continue to pray for the individual and their healing.

**Proverbs 18:19** *A brother offended is harder to win than a strong city, and contentions are like the bars of a castle.*

This verse illustrates the monumental task that sometimes confronts you and stands before you. There are times when you will feel like a mountain climber who is crossing the Himalayas without oxygen. You must remember God looks at the condition of the heart and not at the resulting action, successes, failures, or results of your works done in faith. God knows the condition of the heart involved, and you must trust Him completely with the circumstances and outcome that results from your actions, even when your desired results are not accomplished. You must remain open to trying and not become discouraged or frustrated if reconciliation does not take place right away. The lack of immediate reconciliation does not remove your responsibility to continue trying. You must remain steadfast through prayer, fasting, and the pursuit of His will. You must not shrink back from the desired goal. God told you that you would be rewarded if you diligently sought after Him and that reward is assured, whether it is presented to you in this lifetime or the one to come.

If there is a willingness for reconciliation in your heart and you have sought after forgiveness from this individual and they still continue to refuse to forgive, then the law of love would yield to the wishes of the individual—despite the hurt, pain, and confusion it causes you.

A word of warning needs to be stated here. The desire for reconciliation will be great within your heart, and you must be on guard that your newfound zeal does not become a weapon for the enemy to use against you. When there is a lack of forgiveness and reconciliation, it leaves a vacuum that could be replaced or filled with fear, anger, and the desire to isolate and reject the individual who refuses to reconcile with you. You must be willing to forgive an individual who refuses to forgive and reconcile with you, no matter how much you desire it.

You cannot demand forgiveness anymore than you can demand reconciliation. You cannot ask for forgiveness and reconciliation like this, "I need to confess some things to you and I want you to forgive me and reconcile with me right now." Remember it is asking for, not demanding of. The actions and results of these two powerful gifts are a result of grace and time. Therefore, you must be aware of the possibility of bitterness in your own heart. It can begin to grow at the moment you become disappointed, discouraged, or sinned against.

**Matthew 13:28-30** *"He said to them, 'An enemy has done this.' The servants said to him, 'Do you want us then to go and gather them up?' But he said, 'No, lest while you gather up the tares you also uproot the wheat with them. Let both grow together until the harvest, and at the time of harvest I will say to the reapers, "First gather together the tares and bind them in bundles to burn them, but gather the wheat into my barn."*

You must be aware of the potential that there will be occasions when you will have to wait for all the weeds to grow up within the wheat you have planted.

There may be delays in your ability to make peace and sow harmony with your fellow brethren. However, that should not be a deterrent to your obedience to the will of God for you to reconcile. If these times present themselves for you to deal with, you can trust with full assurance in your heart God's purposes and counsel are far greater than your own. You can rest upon His promise, **Ecclesiastes 3:11**, *"He has made everything beautiful in its time…."* If you will focus upon Him and hope in Him, you will have the peace you so desperately desire and need. **Isaiah 26:3**, *"You will keep him in perfect peace, whose mind is stayed on You, because he trusts in You."*

**Principle 8 - *I MAKE A LIST OF ALL PERSONS I HAVE HARMED AND BECOME WILLING AND READY TO MAKE AMENDS WITH THEM WHEN GOD GIVES ME THE OPPORTUNITY TO DO SO.***

First, you make a list of people God has revealed to you by doing the previous principles. Second, you "become willing and ready" to make amends. This is an example of your faith at work by its manifestation <u>in your will</u> to make amends despite your fears of the unknown. This work of <u>love for God that is in your heart and will</u> is manifest through <u>your obedience to Him</u>, rather than a feeling or desire to do so.

While compiling your list, you should keep in mind those you have harmed by "word and deed" and by "sins of omission." You need to ask God to help you to recognize your unforgiveness and bitterness since these are sins, and these have been the cause of trouble and tribulation in your life. You also need to list those who have hurt and harmed you, as they need forgiveness from your heart. You understand that in some of these areas there may still be a great deal of pain, but God desires for you to trust Him so He can heal you and bring resolution and reconciliation to all areas in your life.

**Proverbs 14:9** *Fools mock at sin, but among the upright there is favor.* (NKJV) *Fools mock at making amends for sin, but goodwill is found among the upright.* (NIV)

The word <u>fool</u> means *one who despises wisdom, one who mocks when guilty, one who is quarrelsome, one who is licentious* (OLB). Licentious is being lawless or immoral; it is going beyond customary or proper bounds or limits. It is disregarding rules. This type of person <u>mocks</u> (*to be inflated, talk arrogantly, scoff, act as a scorner, to deride* (OLB)).

The fool ridicules the meaning of sin.

**Sin:** Sin means *to offend, be guilty, trespass, to do wrong, commit an offense, do injury, to be or become guilty, to be held guilty, to be incriminated, to suffer punishment, to declare guilty, to be desolate, and to acknowledge offense (OLB).*

The cause of this attitude and mindset is arrogance. Arrogance is defined in the scriptures in **Revelation 3:17**, *"Because you say, 'I am rich, have become wealthy, and have need of nothing' —and do not know that you are wretched, miserable, poor, blind, and naked."* This truth is also spelled out in **1 Corinthians 8:1-2, 10:12**, *"Knowledge puffs up, but love edifies. And if anyone thinks that he knows anything, he knows nothing yet as he ought to know... Therefore let him who thinks he stands take heed lest he fall."*

As you begin to practice these principles and observe these truths, the reasons why you were the way you were will become clear. You'll notice sin is not reserved to just the mental area or your thinking. It also involves your words and your actions. It affects the social, legal, spiritual, and health areas. You see, sin affects your whole life. You now know you cannot mock the evidence of sin and the works it has produced and promoted in your life. The NIV translates the desire to make amends as "good will."

**1 John 2:9-11** *He who says he is in the light, and hates his brother, is in darkness until now. He who loves his brother abides in the light, and there is no cause for stumbling in him. But he who hates his brother is in darkness and walks in darkness, and does not know where he is going, because the darkness has blinded his eyes.*

In these verses you see the contrast between the way you used to live and the newly developed desire and direction you have now. Because of self-deception, it was easy for you to state to yourself, as well as to others, that you were in the light. Your self-justification gave you reason that it was okay to hate or hold resentments against others. You see the truth as revealed here—you were still in darkness.

God is mentioned in two different ways – as love and light. The Apostle John states the LORD is love. **1 John 4:8**, "*He who does not love does not know God, for God is love.*" Both John and Jesus, Himself, stated He was the light of men and life. **John 1:4**, "*In Him was life, and the life was the light of men.*" **John 8:12**, "*Then Jesus spoke to them again, saying, 'I am the light of the world. He who follows Me shall not walk in darkness, but have the light of life.'*"

The Apostle also states when you are walking in God's love, there is no cause for stumbling. Your conscience will be your guide and witness. The Holy Spirit will be able to truly lead and direct you. This does not mean love will not cause stumbling. Remember love caused the biggest stumbling in history in that your sins were the cause for the murder of God's Son. Love does stumble sinners, and love is very misunderstood by those of the world.

This simply means the light of love illuminates your way and draws you towards holiness and purity. It causes you to yearn for peace and unity. *Pursue peace with all people, and holiness, without which no one will see the Lord:… This is the message which we have heard from Him and declare to you, that God is light and in Him is no darkness at all… But if we walk in the light as He is in the light, we have fellowship with one another, and the blood of Jesus Christ His Son cleanses us from all sin… And everyone who has this hope in Him purifies himself, just as He is pure… If it is possible, as much as depends on you, live peaceably with all men… Therefore let us pursue the things which make for peace and the things by which one may edify another… Now the fruit of righteousness is sown in peace by those who make peace… I, therefore, the prisoner of the Lord, beseech you to walk worthy of the calling with which you were called, with all lowliness and gentleness, with longsuffering, bearing with one another in love, endeavoring to keep the unity of the Spirit in the bond of peace… Behold, how good and how pleasant it is for brethren to dwell together in unity!*

If you are in the truth and in the light, you will have a pure desire to have God reconcile you with those whom He has revealed to your heart. If He is leading you, you will be able to overcome <u>all</u> hindrances that would stand in the way of making peace between you. This includes those hindrances that stealthily hide in the depths of your heart such as pride, bitterness, envy, unforgiveness, and your will.

Love is always in the light; hate is a work of darkness. You see not only is the brother who hates in the darkness, he also is walking in the darkness. This is contrary to walking in the light or the Spirit. The Apostle Paul stated in **Galatians 5:16**, "*Walk in the Spirit, and you shall not fulfill the lust of the flesh.*" He also stated the fruit of the Spirit consisted of this nature, **Galatians 5:22**, "*… love, joy, peace, longsuffering, kindness, goodness, faithfulness, gentleness, self-control.*" So, if you are in Him and He is lighting the way, you will have His nature influencing you. As the scripture says, **1 John 1:7**, "*But if we walk in the light as He is in the light, we have fellowship with one another, and the blood of Jesus Christ His Son cleanses us from all sin.*"

This verse also points out if you are in the darkness, you won't know where you are going. Have you ever found yourself in the dark? What does it do to your confidence? What happens to your fear level? What happens to your balance? What happens to your pain level? Doesn't it hurt more to stumble in the dark than it does in the light?

**Matthew 7:12** *Therefore, whatever you want men to do to you, do also to them, for this is the Law and the Prophets.*

This verse (and Luke 6:31) declare the golden rule for living. It shows you how far off the mark you truly are. You would think treating others just like you would like to be treated wouldn't be a big deal, but how many of you can truly state with a clean and unconvicted conscience that you have? The truth is you haven't. You are usually so self-centered and selfish you never stop to think about how you are treating others, especially while you are motivated by fear and in the pursuit of your own desires.

What Principle 8 does for you when it is properly appropriated in your life is to help you develop a balance between reconciliation and restitution. It prepares your heart and mind to accept the fact this action needs to take place out of obedience, <u>not feeling</u>. It begins to help you practice a willingness to yield to the mighty hand of God. It prepares your heart to put your trust in Him and to believe He does want the best for you and all those in your life. This principle will take time to develop, and the works done in faith will have the most powerful effect of all the things you'll do. It will not only show you the power of grace in your life, but it will show others also. Others will see the work of God in a way they would never have believed, and they will know there is a God when He continues to change you in a consistent manner. The change will be so profound there will be no other explanation for the success. One day all praise will go to Him and Him alone!

**Mark 11:25-26** *And whenever you stand praying, if you have anything against anyone, forgive him, that your Father in heaven may also forgive you your trespasses. But if you do not forgive, neither will your Father in heaven forgive your trespasses.* (Compare with Matthew 6:14-15.)

You finish Principle 8 with the reminder once again that forgiveness is the most important thing that can transpire in your heart and be given in life. In the last lesson, you read a verse that stated if you truthfully realize how much you have been forgiven, you will not hesitate to forgive as graciously as you have been forgiven. It was about a woman who had many sins, **Luke 7:47**, *"Therefore I say to you, her sins, which are many, are forgiven, for she loved much. But to whom little is forgiven, the same loves little."* Principle 8 points out the need of having both your heart and your will lined up with God's Word so you can forgive completely and practice forgiving quickly. Remember, the more you practice forgiving, the better you'll get at it. Remember, practice makes perfect. So, practice, practice, and practice!!

Principle 9 is the balance point to all the zeal you now have developed with the fruit, progress, and the success you see manifesting in your life. There will be times you will desire to be reconciled for all the right reasons and out of desires from a pure heart, but will be thwarted by the enemy, as well as the other individual's heart. Many reasons could be listed here. Suffice it to say when these occasions arise, you must be guided by love and must be willing to yield to the interests of others, not your own. You must be willing to persevere through prayer for the desired results, even when you know it would be the best thing to have an immediate resolution to the hurt, pain, and problem.

**Principle 9 - *I MAKE DIRECT AMENDS TO SUCH PEOPLE, WHENEVER POSSIBLE, EXCEPT WHEN TO DO SO WOULD INJURE THEM OR OTHERS.***

You make amends to people in many different ways. If you owe them money, pay them back. If you have hurt them or insulted them, you apologize and repent. If people have harmed you, you forgive them. You do whatever you must in order to be at peace with your fellow man. By doing so, you begin to have peace in your heart, soul, and conscience, and most importantly, you have peace with your heavenly Father. You find when you hold resentments against someone or withhold something you owe to someone, you cannot walk in "freedom" because you are then spiritually united to that person and held in bondage to that debt by your conscience.

There may be some people you have harmed that you are unable to make amends to; perhaps they have died or moved away. In these cases, you will make amends by helping your fellow man. Since Jesus told you, "If I do good to my neighbor I am doing good to Him," you are then making amends to God. You may feel your brother needs to make amends to you before you grant forgiveness, but in God's plan, you must be the first to obey and be willing to seek reconciliation because this is the way of love. The result of your obedience to His will and Word are manifested in the work God does in your heart and your will.

**Matthew 5:23-24** *Therefore, if you bring your gift to the altar, and there remember that your brother has something against you, leave your gift there before the altar, and go your way. First be reconciled to your brother, and then come and offer your gift.*

This scripture states you need to keep God's perspective in all you do. You can do this because of the indwelling of the Holy Spirit within you. As you continue to pray, keep your heart open to His influence and guidance, and continue to work with those whom He has sovereignly placed within your life, you can be assured you will accomplish His will with the least amount of pain and suffering in the lives of others, as well as your own.

In the second verse, you see the need for patience and endurance to run this race. It states you can get all the way to the altar and there be hindered by the reminder of the Holy Spirit to go to that person and try to make amends. You are to be obedient, leave your gift at the altar, and then not worry about someone else using it or stealing it or anything of the like—God will take care of it. You are just to leave it, then go and try to reconcile. Notice it doesn't give a time limit for this process. It just gives you a simple procedure, which is to seek reconciliation.

**Luke 20:25** *And He said to them, "Render therefore to Caesar the things that are Caesar's, and to God the things that are God's."*

God says the world has its own agenda and set of standards and the Kingdom of God and the world do not mix. It shows God is not a selfish God and gives liberally to all men, even when it means it is death these men of the world choose. Caesar could have all that was his even though the truth was that it was only on loan from God. Jesus wasn't threatened by the lie Caesar believed. He wasn't threatened by another king or the possibility of another king. Jesus knew His kingdom wasn't of this world, and He would be given all things in the end. (Philippians 2:5-8; John 18:36; Luke 10:22; Psalms 24:1; 50:10; Acts 17:25)

So, what if the person you have harmed will not forgive or will not allow you to make restitution? What happens if the person has moved and their address cannot be obtained? What happens if the person has died? Does this mean you cannot obtain forgiveness from your heavenly Father and LORD?

You must remember God knows the heart of both you and the offended. If you have done all that is possible, if you have done all He has laid on your heart to do, if you have sacrificed your will in these matters and had Him conform your will to His, you will have your forgiveness. This could include writing a letter to the deceased or missing person as though you were speaking to them. It could also consist of acting out a scenario of repentance with them. If this is the case, you will have your forgiveness if you have confessed the same to God and asked Him for forgiveness.

**Romans 13:7-8** *Render therefore to all their due: taxes to whom taxes are due, customs to whom customs, fear to whom fear, honor to whom honor. Owe no one anything except to love one another, for he who loves another has fulfilled the law.*

As previously stated, all things are owned by God and, therefore, you owe God your will and obedience to forgive. Here again you see the will of God is to obey the laws of the land and to render all it requires. You see all God requires you to do is to love one another. He gave that simple command during His last evening and supper with His disciples. **John 13:34**, *"A new commandment I give to you, that you love one another; as I have loved you, that you also love one another. By this all will know that you are My disciples, if you have love for one another."* You are told in another passage that love is perfection, **Colossians 3:14**, *"But above all these things put on love, which is the bond of perfection."*

Your character will change, and you will desire to be conformed and transformed into the image of Christ. The Psalmist states it like this, **Psalms 17:15**, *"As for me, I will see Your face in righteousness; I shall be satisfied when I awake in Your likeness."* You will hunger and thirst for righteousness and you will be filled. **Matthew 5:6**, *"Blessed are those who hunger and thirst for righteousness, for they shall be filled."* You will experience true peace at the moment your will is in line with His.

**Proverbs 25:21-22** *If your enemy is hungry, give him bread to eat; and if he is thirsty, give him water to drink; for so you will heap coals of fire on his head, and the LORD will reward you.*

God always gives you practical help when He is instructing you in His holiness. Here He gives a practical application of mercy. In biblical times, fire was man's only source of heat. Here is the application of love by "heaping hot coals" on your enemy's head. This verse has nothing to do with heavenly revenge, as so many think or desire. God doesn't suddenly switch boats in the middle of the stream. He remains the same, never changing.

Community fires were located in the center of the villages in those times. Someone would always be tending the fire for cooking or heating the homes. After a long day in the fields, one might need to go to the community fire to get some hot coals to take home. He would go to the community fire, grab some hot coals and put some in a basket on his head, and begin his journey home. If he didn't put enough coals in his basket, his coals would go out before he got home. Therefore, if you saw your enemy passing by and you thought this might be a possibility, you were to stop your enemy and place some of your own hot coals in the basket, thus assuring he would arrive home with enough coals to start a fire of his own.

# Conclusion

**1 Peter 3:13-14** *And who is he who will harm you if you become followers of what is good? But even if you should suffer for righteousness' sake, you are blessed. "And do not be afraid of their threats, nor be troubled."*

If you persevere in doing right, you will overcome the persecution that is promised. You are to conduct yourself in such a way that it brings conviction to those who practice darkness. **Ephesians 5:11, 13**, *"And have no fellowship with the unfruitful works of darkness, but rather expose them…. But all things that are exposed are made manifest by the light, for whatever makes manifest is light."* Your good behavior will result, first, in persecution because of the contrast in direction and second, in conviction of the hearts surrounding you because they will be affected by their consciences and will hate the light fearing their exposure (John 3:20).

However, this should not deter you from your goal because if you will persevere, you will overcome and their hearts will be changed because of the mighty works of God done through you. God told you He would be your protector, your shield, and your provider. *"And I say to you, My friends, do not be afraid of those who kill the body, and after that have no more that they can do. But I will show you whom you should fear: fear Him who, after He has killed, has power to cast into hell; yes, I say to you, fear Him!... Hear my voice, O God, in my meditation; preserve my life from fear of the enemy… Because he has set his love upon Me, therefore I will deliver him; I will set him on high, because he has known My name... The LORD shall preserve you from all evil; He shall preserve your soul… As for God, His way is perfect. The word of the LORD is proven; He is a shield to all who trust in Him... You have also given me the shield of Your salvation; Your gentleness has made me great... Our soul waits for the LORD; He is our help and our shield... Take hold of shield and buckler, and stand up for my help... Help us, O God of our salvation, for the glory of Your name; and deliver us, and provide atonement for our sins, For Your name's sake!.. The God of my strength, in whom I will trust; my shield and the horn of my salvation, my stronghold and my refuge; my Savior, You save me from violence… Therefore I say to you, do not worry about your life, what you will eat or what you will drink; nor about your body, what you will put on. Is not life more than food and the body more than clothing? Look at the birds of the air, for they neither sow nor reap nor gather into barns; yet your heavenly Father feeds them. Are you not of more value than they? Which of you by worrying can add one cubit to his stature? So why do you worry about clothing? Consider the lilies of the field, how they grow: they neither toil nor spin; and yet I say to you that even Solomon in all his glory was not arrayed like one of these. Now if God so clothes the grass of the field, which today is, and tomorrow is thrown into the oven, will He not much more clothe you, O you of little faith? Therefore do not worry, saying, 'What shall we eat?' or 'What shall we drink?' or 'What shall we wear?' for after all these things the Gentiles seek. For your heavenly Father knows that you need all these things. But seek first the kingdom of God and His righteousness, and all these things shall be added to you."*

With these things in mind, you can have confidence God will provide all that is needed for your walk in this maturing process of sobriety. This includes your obedience and your change of heart and will.

- 62 -

# Questions for Lesson 5

1.  Why do you naturally desire reconciliation?

2.  What are you to do when someone won't be reconciled with you?

3.  What does fool mean?

4.  What does licentious mean?

5.  What does mock mean?

6.  What does sin mean?

7.  What is the scriptural definition of arrogance?

8.  What is the difference between love and hate?

9.  What is the purpose of Principle 8 and what does it do for your life?

10. According to Matthew 5:23-24, you now have God's perspective in all you do. What enables you to have this precious power? How does your will fit into this process?

11. What if the person will not forgive or will not allow you to make restitution? What happens if the person has moved or died? Does this mean you cannot obtain forgiveness from your heavenly Father and LORD?

12. What will your good behavior cause in those around you who do not believe in God?

# Light in my Heart

I grew up in a dysfunctional family where my parents gave me too much freedom to do as I pleased. Their philosophy was, "We learn by our mistakes." When I was younger, I was sexually abused for years. I watched a good friend of mine die in a skateboarding accident and not more than six months later waited for nine days in the hospital for my older brother to pass away from a fatal motorcycle accident.

These traumatizing incidents in my youth sprang forth eight years of chemical destruction. I was introduced to marijuana and alcohol at 12. With these two mind-altering chemicals I found out I could change the way I felt in a particular situation within moments. By eighth grade, I was drinking and/or smoking pot daily. Wearing nice clothes, having good grades, and excellent composure, I fooled my family as well as most my friends about my secret lifestyle.

It was my first year of high school at 15 when my drug use took a severe turn for the worst. Curious about what other drugs could do with no fear of the repercussions, I wandered out into the world of narcotics. I quickly became addicted to methamphetamines and began distributing to support my ever-growing habit. Within three years I had seen my fair share of meth labs, violent beatings, and guns put pointblank to my head.

I decided this lifestyle was going to kill me if I didn't make a change soon. I quit cold turkey and found myself in convulsions at school 16 hours later. At the hospital, the doctors informed me that at my heavy use rate, I would have to cut back in increments to avoid shock to my system. That's when I checked into the Walker Center of Gooding, Idaho. In 27 days, I came out of the Walker Center with a new light in my heart—God.

I finally had a reason to live; God touched me so deeply in Gooding, Idaho, and I have never touched meth since. I came out with love in my heart and a purpose for my life. I found my new church family at Calvary Chapel Boise where I was quickly accepted and found new friends.

I attend church three times a week, which keeps a healthy, sane head on my shoulders. I work full time and attend school at Boise State University full time. I smile and laugh and experience emotions I thought I lost permanently. Best of all, I'm SOBER! God has made such a significant change in my heart and life; I can only imagine where I would be at right now without Him. And that's not a pretty sight.

Thank you God,
Your servant for life

# Lesson 6: The Importance of Keeping Accounts Small, Principle 10

To begin Principle 10, review the process you have already completed or at least have begun. You have come through the first four principles of accepting your responsibilities in all of your actions and because of the grace, mercy, and forgiveness working in your heart, you now know your need to forgive and be as merciful, in as much as you have been given mercy. Your new zeal has given you the desire to make amends and reconcile with others as much as depends upon you. Now you have grown to the place of maturity in your life that causes you to keep your personal relationship accounts in a clean and orderly manner with God. Principle 10 helps you to do just that. The first verse that makes this point for you comes from the letter to the Romans.

**Romans 6:11** *Likewise you also, reckon yourselves to be dead indeed to sin, but alive to God in Christ Jesus our Lord.*

The word <u>reckon</u> means *to count, compute, calculate; to reckon inward, weigh the reasons, to deliberate; meditate on; to suppose, deem, judge; to determine* (OLB). This word deals with reality. If you reckon your bankbook has $25 in it, it has $25 in it. Otherwise, you are deceiving yourself. This word refers to facts, not suppositions.

You are to reckon yourself dead to sin. This is a fact, not a rumor or theory. It is the reality of the matter, not a feeling. You are to place a zero in the personal cost column, the ledger column of debt, which keeps the total wage of your sins as zero. It has been paid by the sacrifice of your Savior Jesus Christ. In your behalf, your heavenly Father has accounted the cost of your sins to the ledger of His Son. Your debt to God is now zero, nadda, nothing, zip. Jesus paid it all for you.

By doing this on a daily basis, you are able to keep your conscience clean, alert, and sensitive to the direction and guidance of the Holy Spirit. You are to be filled with and kept under the control of the Holy Spirit. This enables you to walk in the Spirit. If God's attributes are yours, you will be more sensitive to the love of the Father and the conviction of the Holy Spirit. He will be able to correct you and lead you into righteousness.

Principle 10 continues to establish the foundation you have been endeavoring to build. Thus far, you have established God's <u>perspective</u> when it comes to your sin. He has shown you the reasons for your <u>hope</u> because of the promises of forgiveness and redemption. In doing so, you now have the directions for your God-given <u>change</u>. In the remaining three principles, you will look at the last of the directives God gives you, and hopefully, these will become your daily <u>practice</u>.

The first practice of this last phase is to take a daily inventory. This will help you to remain sensitive to the will of God and will help you to practice holiness. Because of this practice, you will then be able to surrender to the desires of God and will be able to discern His will. You will become more sensitive to His voice and your relationship with Him and others will be alive, enhanced, and active. The final two phases will concentrate on prayer and service, but before you get to those principles you have to make sure your relationship is clean before God. The way you will accomplish this is to do a daily inventory and prepare your heart for seeking the face of God through prayer and then being sent out according to His will, to accomplish His tasks by grace through faith.

**Principle 10 - *I CONTINUE TO TAKE PERSONAL INVENTORIES, AND WHEN I AM WRONG, I PROMPTLY ADMIT IT.***

If you are to live for Christ, you must continue to grow and mature in Him. This is His sole responsibility, and it is accomplished through the process called sanctification. Sanctification is not a series of growth spurts, but a continuous and steady process into holiness. If you do not continue to grow, mature, or experience the ongoing blessing of an abundant life in the Lord Jesus Christ, you will become fearful of change and become stagnant, stunted, or enter into a relapse condition.

There are great blessings and a newfound freedom in the ability to admit to God and others when you are wrong. It is a great discovery when you find out you do not always have to be right. When you speak God's Word, you hopefully speak truth in love and with great power to heal. When you speak your words, you are sometimes wrong and inflict great wounds and, sometimes, irreparable harm. In such cases, you are to promptly admit it and to seek forgiveness and reconciliation (Matthew 5:23-24). This will eliminate the chances of bitterness, resentment, guilt, shame, or a record of wrongs to grow within your heart and conscience.

Remember, as long as you reside in the light and live and grow in it, God will continue to reveal the areas in your life that must be cleansed. The Apostle Paul said if you would judge yourself you would not be judged (1 Corinthians 11:31). As these areas or incidents arise, you will learn to confess them and ask the Lord and others for forgiveness. The evidence of your forgiveness will result in your acts of turning away from these practices, habits, or patterns.

**1 Peter 1:22-23** *Since you have purified your souls in obeying the truth through the Spirit in sincere love of the brethren, love one another fervently with a pure heart, having been born again, not of corruptible seed but incorruptible, through the word of God which lives and abides forever...*

Here is the process in which you have purified your soul, and this was accomplished through the simple act of obedience. When the season of time arrives that you begin to practice applying this principle to your life, you will have already established the habit of obeying and listening to the Holy Spirit and applying what you have read and learned in the Word of God. This obedience was refined through reading and application of the truth of God's Word to your life on a daily basis. It also tells you it is enabled and empowered by the Spirit through the love of others, not through the love of self. This principle helps keep your love fervent, and as you stay in the light that is shed by the Word into your heart, you see the remaining result, which is a pure heart.

The result of new birth is an incorruptible life that is sealed in God, not in yourself, and yields to the Word of God, which is alive and active. It also abides forever and is thought of as being more valuable than gold, as well as being revered higher than God's name. (Psalms 119:72; 119:89; 138:2; Isaiah 40:8; Matthew 5:18; 24:35; 2 Corinthians 1:21-22; Ephesians 1:12-13; 2 Timothy 2:19)

**Psalms 119:127** *Therefore, I love Your commandments more than gold, yes, than fine gold!*

**Hebrews 4:12** *For the word of God is living and powerful, and sharper than any two-edged sword, piercing even to the division of soul and spirit, and of joints and marrow, and is a discerner of the thoughts and intents of the heart.*

The Word will establish an unshakable foundation of faith and power within you and will do the work required to bless you and keep you. God and His grace are the only things that will continue to cause you to hunger and thirst for His righteousness. They alone will change your heart and desire to be conformed to the image of His Son. Then and only then will His will be the desire of your heart.

**Ephesians 4:25-27** *Therefore, putting away lying, "Let each one of you speak truth with his neighbor," for we are members of one another. "Be angry, and do not sin": do not let the sun go down on your wrath, nor give place to the devil.*

These verses tell you the value of having an honest relationship with your neighbors.

**Lying:**    That which is false or fake. It is untruthfulness, deception, misrepresentation, and/or exaggeration. A lie does three things. 1) It misrepresents the truth, and it camouflages or hides the truth. 2) Lying deceives a person. It leads a person astray. It causes you to deceive or manipulate to get what you want. You lie to seduce someone for your selfish gratification. You lie to cover up or hide something (self-preservation and self-reliance). It also causes harm or hurt. There is no such thing as a white lie or little itsy-bitsy lie. 3) Lying builds a wrong or false relationship, a faulty foundation, a relationship built upon sinking sand. Lying erodes and eventually destroys trust, confidence, love, assurance, security, hope, and lastly, faith. (1 Timothy 1:9-10)

**Revelation 21:8** *But the cowardly, unbelieving, abominable, murderers, sexually immoral, sorcerers, idolaters, and all liars shall have their part in the lake which burns with fire and brimstone, which is the second death.*

You are told to speak the truth to each other because lying causes death to transpire between two individuals. Remember, there is power in the tongue and words can cause harm. The following scriptural examples show you the positive and the negative. (Proverbs 18:21; James 3:6; Proverbs 15:23; Proverbs 16:24)

**James 3:8** *But no man can tame the tongue. It is an unruly evil, full of deadly poison.*

**Proverbs 12:18** *There is one who speaks like the piercings of a sword, but the tongue of the wise promotes health.*

You are told all are one body and everyone has an effect on one another. When your body parts lie to each other, they can be identified as cancer, and they become cancerous. Cancer hides in all of you, and what makes it active is unknown. What makes cancer so dangerous is the fact that none of your other body cells can identify it to fight against it. Your immune system is defenseless against it. Cancer goes undetected, and it camouflages itself until it invades a healthy cell. It then destroys the healthy life. The newly infected cell then turns to another healthy cell, then invades and infects it.

Another example would be the brain; it must have truth in the signals it sends and receives. It must send truthful signals to the different body parts. If it doesn't—it convulses, spasms, or has seizures.

**John 8:44** *You are of your father the devil, and the desires of your father you want to do. He was a murderer from the beginning, and does not stand in the truth, because there is no truth in him. When he speaks a lie, he speaks from his own resources, for he is a liar and the father of it.*

Lastly, you see the father and author of lies. You used to be under his control as a slave and without choice. He manipulated, ruled, and governed you. Now, you have been delivered and set free and have freedom to choose whom you will serve—the flesh or the Spirit.

**1 Corinthians 13:4-8a** *Love suffers long and is kind; love does not envy; love does not parade itself, is not puffed up; does not behave rudely, does not seek its own, is not provoked, thinks no evil; does not rejoice in iniquity, but rejoices in the truth; bears all things, believes all things, hopes all things, endures all things. Love never fails.*

Principle 10 keeps you operating in the realm of truthfulness. <u>It makes you exercise your conscience on a daily basis</u>. If you are in the light, you will live and conduct yourself in the light. You won't operate in fear, and you won't fear being exposed. Your growth and maturity will manifest and be obvious to those who surround you.

Principle 10 also causes you to grow in love. Love is the power of the Christian's walk and life. In the letter to the Romans (12:9-21) you see the <u>action of love</u>. In the letter to the Galatians (5:22-23) you see the <u>nature of love</u>. In these next verses in the first letter to the Corinthians (13:4-8a), you see the <u>character of love</u>.

## The Meaning of Biblical Love

The primary meaning of the word love in Scripture is a purposeful commitment to sacrificial action for another. In fact, loving God is demonstrated by obeying His Word (John 14:15, 21, 23-24; 1 John 5:3; 2 John 1:6). Powerful emotions may accompany biblical love, but it is the commitment of the will that holds love steadfast and unchanging. Emotions may change, but a commitment to love in a biblical manner endures and is the hallmark of a disciple of Jesus Christ (John 3:16, 13:34-35; Romans 5:8-11; 1 Corinthians 13:4-8a, 13).

Love has specific characteristics demonstrated by godly deeds (thoughts, words, and actions) (1 Corinthians 13:4-8a). The test of biblical love is to do the following, especially when you don't feel like it (Matthew 5:46-48).

1. **LOVE IS PATIENT**, *even when you feel like forcefully expressing yourself.* Love bears pain or trials without complaint, shows forbearance under provocation or strain, and is steadfast despite opposition, difficulty, or adversity.

2. **LOVE IS KIND**, *even when you want to retaliate physically or tear down another with your words.* Love is sympathetic, considerate, gentle, and agreeable.

3. **LOVE IS NOT JEALOUS**, *especially when you are aware that others are being noticed more than you.* Love does not participate in rivalry, is not hostile toward one believed to enjoy an advantage, and is not suspicious. Love works for the welfare and good of the other.

4. **LOVE DOES NOT BRAG**, *even when you want to tell the world about your accomplishments.* Love does not flaunt itself boastfully and does not engage in self-glorification. Instead, love lifts (builds up) others.

5. **LOVE IS NOT ARROGANT**, *even when you think you are right and others are wrong.* Love does not assert itself or become overbearing in dealing with others.

6. **LOVE DOES NOT ACT UNBECOMINGLY**, *even when being boastful, rude, or overbearing will get you attention and allow you to get your own way.* Love conforms to what is right, fitting, and appropriate to the situation in order to honor the Lord.

7. **LOVE DOES NOT SEEK ITS OWN**, *even when you feel like grabbing it all or have an opportunity to do so.* Love does not try to fulfill its own desires, does not ask for its own way, and does not try to acquire gain for itself. Love, as an act of the will, seeks to serve and not to be served.

8. **LOVE IS NOT PROVOKED**, *even when others attempt to provoke you or you are tempted to strike out at something or someone.* Love is not aroused or incited to outbursts of anger. Love continues faithfully and gently to train others in righteousness, even when they fail.

9. **LOVE DOES NOT TAKE INTO ACCOUNT A WRONG SUFFERED**, *even when everyone seems to be against you or when people openly attack you.* Love does not hold a grudge against someone. Love forgives, chooses not to bring up past wrongs in accusation or retaliation, does not return evil for evil, and does not indulge in self-pity. Love covers a multitude of sins.

10. **LOVE DOES NOT REJOICE IN UNRIGHTEOUSNESS**, *even when it seems like a misfortune was exactly what another person deserved.* Love mourns over sin, its effects, and the pain which results from living in a fallen world. Love seeks to reconcile others with the Lord.

11. **LOVE REJOICES WITH THE TRUTH**, *even when it is easier and more profitable, materially, to lie.* Love is joyful when truth is known, even when it may lead to adverse circumstances, reviling, or persecution.

12. **LOVE BEARS ALL THINGS**, *even when disappointments seem overwhelming.* Love is tolerant, endures with others who are difficult to understand or deal with, and has an

eternal perspective in difficulties. Love remembers that God develops spiritual maturity through difficult circumstances.

13. **LOVE BELIEVES ALL THINGS**, *even when others' actions are ambiguous and you feel like not trusting anyone.* Love accepts trustfully, does not judge people's motives, and believes others until facts prove otherwise. Even when facts prove that the other person is untrustworthy, love seeks to help restore the other to trustworthiness.

14. **LOVE HOPES ALL THINGS**, *even when nothing appears to be going right.* Love expects fulfillment of God's plan and anticipates the best for the other person. Love confidently entrusts others to the Lord to do His sovereign and perfect will in their lives.

15. **LOVE ENDURES ALL THINGS**, *especially when you think you just can't endure the people or circumstances in your life.* Love remains steadfast under suffering or hardship without yielding and returns a blessing while undergoing trials.

16. **LOVE NEVER FAILS**, *even when you feel overwhelmed and the situation seems hopeless.* Love will not crumble under pressure or difficulties. Love remains selflessly faithful, even to the point of death.

The portion 'Love Is' is copied from pages 217 to 219 in the Self-Confrontation manual, which is written and published by the Biblical Counseling Foundation (BCF). Although BCF has granted permission to copy this portion from their materials, this does not imply that the Biblical Counseling Foundation is in agreement with the other portions of this work, nor is BCF in any other way associated with this organization. The Biblical Counseling Foundation does not receive monetary gain from the sale of this workbook.

You have a long way to go but this is the mark you must aim for. May you not be discouraged in doing well. God will bless your efforts, and you must not shrink back just because it gets hard or uncomfortable. When the vice of love squeezes you, it produces more grace from within you.

**Philippians 2:1-4** *Therefore if there is any consolation in Christ, if any comfort of love, if any fellowship of the Spirit, if any affection and mercy, 2 fulfill my joy by being like-minded, having the same love, being of one accord, of one mind. 3 Let nothing be done through selfish ambition or conceit, but in lowliness of mind let each esteem others better than himself. 4 Let each of you look out not only for his own interests, but also for the interests of others.*

Here Paul addresses the reason to do an inventory on a daily basis. In verse 1, he states there are four things that persuade you.

1. If there be any <u>consolation</u> in Christ, which means *a calling near, exhortation, admonition, encouragement, solace, that which affords comfort or refreshment* (OLB). You have a calling, and Christ gives you comfort, not complacency.

2. <u>Comfort in love</u>, which means *a persuasive address* (OLB). Remember, the love of Christ constrains or compels you.

3.  <u>Fellowship (koinonia) of the Spirit</u>, which means *fellowship, association, community, communion; joint participation* (OLB).

4.  <u>Affection</u> and <u>mercy</u>. Affection means *seat of the more tender affections: kindness, benevolence, compassion; hence our heart* (OLB). Mercy means *emotions, longings, manifestations of pity* (OLB). Pity is to see a need and to supersede the limit of the needed thing; to give more than is needed in order to meet it. See John 3:16 for an example.

Verse 2 gives you your instructions. You are to be like-minded, having the same love and being united in mind and understanding. If you have a small build-up of resentment or difference of opinion that causes an irritation, you will be hindered from obeying this command. It gives you time to sort out your emotions and enables you to make a balanced judgment about issues or concerns. This principle allows you to confront yourself.

Verse 3 nails your self-centeredness and pride. It tells you that you are not to be assertive or forward. It instructs you not to be <u>conceited</u> (from KJV: *vain glory, groundless, self-esteem, empty pride, a vain opinion, or error* (OLB)). It gives you the correct way of handling things and that is in the mindset of <u>lowliness</u> (*having a humble opinion of one's self, a deep sense of one's (moral) littleness, modesty, humility, and lowliness of mind* (OLB)). The word <u>esteem</u> means *to lead, to go before* (OLB). Therefore, you must take the initiative in making amends because you put others' needs above your own.

Verse 4 continues the same thought and concludes with the fact you love your own interests, and these usually lie in the middle, or core, of your selfishness. In other words, God is telling you here to die to self and allow others to live.

**1 John 1:9** *If we confess our sins, He is faithful and just to forgive us our sins and to cleanse us from all unrighteousness.*

Your confession causes growth and security in both your walk with the Lord, as well as with others. You are shown God holds nothing back from you when it comes to forgiveness. It is once again an example you are told to follow in your own life. You are to forgive as much as you have been forgiven.

**1 John 2:1-2** *My little children, these things I write to you, so that you may not sin. And if anyone sins, we have an Advocate with the Father, Jesus Christ the righteous. And He Himself is the propitiation for our sins, and not for ours only but also for the whole world.*

It also gives you great comfort that in doing an inventory you can rest assured you have your Savior working on your behalf to keep the unity of the Spirit, as well as the body. <u>There will be no condemnation in the work of the Spirit as you do a daily inventory</u>. Your heart will be pure, and your conscience will be clean. Therefore, you will have peace with God and your fellow brethren.

# Conclusion

**James 1:22** *But be doers of the word, and not hearers only, deceiving yourselves.*

The Bible closes with an important warning. James writes the importance of not just listening to these instructions but applying yourself to them. He gives you a warning and expects you to heed it. The meaning of the word <u>deceiving</u> is *to reckon wrong, miscount; to cheat by false reckoning; to deceive by false reasoning; to delude, circumvent* (OLB). Remember, reckon means *to add up and to be factual.* This word refers to facts, not something supposed. You are to apply the Word to your everyday life and not just listen to it at a Sunday morning service or on the radio. Your Lord desires to be intimately involved in your life. Remember, He purchased you and the price tag on you reads "God's only Son" – God's Son was the payment. God didn't hold anything back. He went all the way and left nothing to spare. God's love is whole, complete, and perfect. If you allow Him to have His way with you, you will have this promise from **1 John 3:2**, *"Beloved, now we are children of God; and it has not yet been revealed what we shall be, but we know that when He is revealed, we shall be like Him, for we shall see Him as He is."*

If you, by faith, apply the truths of this principle you have learned and found written in the scriptures, you can be assured you will have peace with your Savior and fellow man. The fruit born from your efforts and works will be given back to you on your "day of rewards" in the form of a crown. In this life, you will grow in favor with both God and man because love will be manifest and obvious as your source of power and your goal in this life.

# Questions for Lesson 6

1. What does reckon mean? How can you apply this meaning to your life now?

2. What makes up the four layers in your foundation for change? Why are these so important to your life within sobriety?

3. What establishes obedience in your new life in Christ? Are your acts of self-discipline good enough to make you sober for the rest of your life?

4. What are the results of a new birth? How do you know it has taken effect in your life? What are some of the obvious changes that have taken place in your life?

5. What are the two things that cause a hunger and thirst for His righteousness?

6. What does lying mean and what does a lie do?

7. Give some examples of how lying has affected you. Be specific.

8. How has the truth affected your sobriety? Write down some specific ways truth has made a difference in your life and walk.

9. What does Principle 10 accomplish and cause you to exercise daily?

10. Where in the scriptures is the action of love described?

11. Where in the scriptures is the nature of love described?

12. Where in the scriptures is the character of love described?

13. What does the vice of love produce within you?

14. What does consolation in Christ mean? What does it mean to you to know God recognizes you and is calling you to come to Him?

15. What does comfort in love mean?

16. What does fellowship of the Spirit mean?

17. What do affection, mercy, and pity mean? Give some examples of where God's definition has been applied to your life lately. What has been the most noticeable difference?

18. What does conceited mean? How does this effect your understanding now of the doctrine of self-esteem?

19. What does lowliness mean?

20. What does esteem mean?




21. What does confession cause to develop within you? Have you been able to see this new change develop in your life? Be specific.




22. What does deceiving mean? How does having your own understanding play into deceiving yourself? Will having God's perspective have an effect on your daily walk of sobriety?

# Sincerely Surrendered

I was born an only child in 1965. My father left my mother when she was pregnant. She remarried a few years later but by the time I was 5, she divorced and it was just the two of us once more. My mother is a good woman but she isn't easy to get along with. She always loved me but was exceedingly overwhelmed by life as a single mother trying to raise an ornery, stubborn, strong-willed child. From what I can remember, I raised myself. Unfortunately, without guidance and discipline or any real moral fiber, by the time I was 13, it was easy to make bad decisions and not be too concerned about consequences because at that time it didn't seem to matter that much. Thirteen was when I was first introduced to marijuana.

With no real identity and low self-esteem, the experience of the high filled a huge void in me that at the time seemed like the answer. Little did I know it would be the beginning of a nightmare that lasted for 27 more years.

I could spend the next year writing about the details of my addiction and the pain I caused myself and countless others, but I won't. I will say that marijuana led me to every other substance imaginable— none of which was more devastating than methamphetamine. Somehow all that stuff—jail, broken relationships, lost jobs, and medical problems—doesn't seem important.

What does matter is how much all of that stuff has changed since I came to the Lord and truly, fully, sincerely surrendered my life to Him. My prayer is these words might break through the pain and suffering and injustices of your life experiences that haunt your memories and rattle around in your head and grip your heart and bring hope, peace, and joy beyond belief as it has in mine. "Hope," you say, "that's just another four-letter word that belongs with all the other words we shouldn't say." I remember when I used to feel that way, but thank the Lord; He's shown me that just isn't so.

Every morning I spend time reading the Bible, and through the day I talk with God just as I'm talking to you now. The joy of living and inexplicable hope and peace that fills my life is beyond my ability to explain. Please don't misunderstand—I don't mean my life is easy and all my problems have been solved. That would be a lie. I will say what used to confuse, anger, and bewilder me in life somehow isn't as difficult or discouraging as it was when I used to try to do it on my own. I can't remember the last time I felt lonely. I can remember before I met the Lord, being surrounded by crowds of people most of whom I knew and never feeling more lonely.

In closing, I would like to thank the Lord for this opportunity to share myself and thank you for the time you spent reading it.

Ray

# Lesson 7: The Importance of Prayer, Principle 11

Before you begin Principle 11, review what you have already studied and have prayerfully begun to live. You have come to deal with your denial on a regular basis because of your growing and developing relationship with God. Lying to others and yourself has ceased to be your practice. Now you realize and recognize the freedom found by living in the light and telling the truth. With the result of confronting your denial, your <u>will</u> now has a desire to be conformed to the image of Christ's will. With the assistance of the Holy Spirit, you are now able to follow and be humbly directed into an abundant life, pleasing to the Lord.

The results of doing an inventory have made way for you to conquer the fear, guilt, shame, and condemnation that had ruled you in the past. The result of discovering the faith and power to move ahead and the ability to confront your past without condemnation have given you a new courage and zeal to continue on your path of righteousness. **Job 10:6**, "*That You should seek for my iniquity and search out my sin,…*"

With the healing that has resulted from allowing God to reveal to you your sins and His graciousness to grant you the ability to repent from them (2 Timothy 2:25-26), you now have within you the desire for full reconciliation with those relationships within your ability to reconcile. With the help of God and His gift of other people by your side, you are now given the desire to clear and clean up those sins that have separated you from your loved ones, friends, and acquaintances. Your conscience is now being healed and sensitized to the voice of God, and your practice of obedience is making your boldness more evident. Because of the newly found sensitivity and conscious awareness of the feelings for others, you now seek out God's will before you act. You are beginning to learn and recognize the fact your reconciliation process is not entirely about you, but is primarily about others. Therefore, you are willing to endure and persevere the tough, lonely times where the ones whom you have hurt are not willing immediately to reconcile. <u>It is God's responsibility to develop the desire in the hearts of others to forgive and reconcile with you.</u> Because of the new work ongoing within you, you now have the ability to suffer and wait for God's season and timing. **Ecclesiastes 3:11**, "*He has made everything beautiful in its time….*"

You have also looked at the first phase of the necessity of keeping your conscience and walk clean. You saw your need of having God's perspective when it comes to your sin. By doing a daily inventory, you are able to surrender to the will of God and practice holiness. You are given the hope and the promise if you are willing and obedient to put into practice these principles, you will be used as a holy vessel in the Master's hand.

Prayer is the second phase in the development of this walk. It is the lifeline of communication and communion. It is the one area that must develop within you in order to have a fruitful and vibrant life. With a living prayer life, you can be assured you can have the desires of your heart because prayer doesn't change things, it changes you. It causes you to learn to listen to His voice. It causes you to distinguish and discern His voice from others that beg for your attention. Prayer teaches you to respond and obey to what you hear Him say. It helps you to learn to surrender to His will, and through practice, you learn to pray for His will to be done, not your own. When you pray for His will through the course of this life, you are promised whatever you ask in His name you will receive.

**Matthew 6:33** *But seek first the kingdom of God and His righteousness, and all these things shall be added to you.*

This verse comes from the Sermon on the Mount. You are told clearly if you first seek the kingdom of God and His righteousness, everything else will come along. This is where faith becomes trust. Do you believe if you truly seek Him, He will take care of the rest? Is this a promise you can truly learn to rest your hat on? You must ask yourself how much time you spend in prayer seeking the things of self, rather than the things of God. Scripture points this truth out to you.

**Philippians 2:21** *For all seek their own, not the things which are of Christ Jesus.*

If this is what your prayer life is like, take some time tonight before you go to sleep. If forgiveness is truly needed now, immediately pray before something causes you to forget what has been presently laid on your heart and conscience to ask for God's forgiveness.

**Matthew 7:7-11** *Ask, and it will be given to you; seek, and you will find; knock, and it will be opened to you. For everyone who asks receives, and he who seeks finds, and to him who knocks it will be opened. Or what man is there among you who, if his son asks for bread, will give him a stone? Or if he asks for a fish, will he give him a serpent? If you then, being evil, know how to give good gifts to your children, how much more will your Father who is in heaven give good things to those who ask Him!*

God tells you to continue to keep asking, keep seeking, and keep knocking. The great thing about God is He always brings a perspective that shows your side of compassion and human nature. Here He shows you that as fathers of this world, you would never give things that were contrary to your nature. He identifies your nature as being evil, but even though you are, you still know what to give. Evil means: *bad, of a bad nature or condition, in a physical sense: diseased or blind. In an ethical sense: wicked, bad* (OLB). You see how your Savior illustrates this truth. If you, being evil in your fallen state of being, can and desire to give good gifts to your children, how much more will your heavenly Father, who is perfect, give good things to His children who ask Him?

**Principle 11 -** *I SOUGHT THROUGH PRAYER AND MEDITATION ON GOD'S WORD TO INCREASE MY FELLOWSHIP WITH HIM, PRAYING CONTINUALLY FOR THE KNOWLEDGE OF HIS WILL FOR ME AND THE POWER OF HIS MIGHT TO ACCOMPLISH IT.*

**James 4:8** states, *"Draw near to God and He will draw near to you."* As you continue to pray and meditate, you will become more attuned to the voice of the Holy Spirit. Someone once said, "Prayer is talking to God and meditation is listening to Him." You meditate by reading God's Word and then think about it, turning it over in your mind until the Holy Spirit reveals its meaning to you.

Once God begins revealing to you what His will for you is in your life, you must continue to seek His direction and the power needed to carry it out. You will discover as you practice this principle how powerfully the Holy Spirit will work in your life and the "Good News of Salvation" will have an ever-increasing reality and value to you.

**Proverbs 4:20-22** *My son, give attention to my words; incline your ear to my sayings. Do not let them depart from your eyes; keep them in the midst of your heart; for they are life to those who find them, and health to all their flesh.*

In this scripture a standard of conduct is laid out for you to heed. You are told to give <u>attention</u> to God's Word. You are to pay attention, become sensitive to, and learn to respond in obedience to its directives. You are also given the word picture of leaning into, to try to listen harder, and by paying closer attention to, through the word incline. You are to focus on God's Word continually and never allow it to depart from your sight. Does this mean you are always to have a Bible in front of your face? It means the eyes of your heart are to be before the Word to steer you from sin.

**Psalms 119:9** *How can a young man cleanse his way? By taking heed according to Your word.*

If you are seeking His will and endeavoring to keep a clean line of communication through prayer, you will keep His Word in the center of your heart. This will be accomplished without effort on your part because this is completed by the Holy Spirit through grace. One of the most pleasing things God loves His children to say back to Him—is His Word.

**Psalms 116:6** *The LORD preserves the simple; I was brought low, and He saved me.*

As you develop and mature, you begin to understand the value of the Word of God. You realize the life it brings to you. Have you ever noticed as you look around at those who have longevity in their walks with the LORD, they all seem young and full of life, even though they may have many years under their belts? The Lord will preserve you. (Psalms 31:23; 97:10; 119:50; 145:20; Proverbs 2:8)

**Ephesians 3:14-19** *For this reason I bow my knees to the Father of our Lord Jesus Christ, from whom the whole family in heaven and earth is named, that He would grant you, according to the riches of His glory, to be strengthened with might through His Spirit in the inner man, that Christ may dwell in your hearts through faith; that you, being rooted and grounded in love, may be able to comprehend with all the saints what is the width and length and depth and height—to know the love of Christ which passes knowledge; that you may be filled with all the fullness of God.*

In these verses, Paul has written a prayer for you to learn. This prayer is not a charm or talisman but an example to follow in regards to the attitude of your heart.

Notice the first thing Paul does from the heart is to bow it before the LORD. He bows his knees to the Father and then gives praise and thanksgiving to the LORD. He is the Creator and the Ruler of all things and deserves your whole worship.

The next thing Paul states is that God would grant to you according to the riches of His glory. How rich is the glory of God? You know it has weight. **2 Corinthians 4:17**, *"For our light affliction, which is but for a moment, is working for us a far more exceeding and eternal weight of glory..."* So how much do you think glory is worth? Priceless! It is a gift from God to you to share and give back to Him. The glory of God is seen and testified of by all who surround you as you learn to walk in Him. It causes praise and thanksgiving to be heard throughout the land. It causes trust to be seen in the unseen and faith to be displayed through the invisible. It gives hope to be had in the impossible and love to be given to the unlovable.

Paul's strength, as does yours, comes from the Holy Spirit, not from within you or from what you do. It is located in your inner man, not in your muscles. It needs to be of the heart, not of the brain. It needs to be of Him, not of you. **Zechariah 4:6**, *"So he answered and said to me: 'This is the word of the LORD to Zerubbabel: "Not by might nor by power, but by My Spirit," says the LORD of hosts.'"*

Christ needs to have a dwelling place within you. It needs to be at the center of your being—not at the top or at the bottom, not on a bookshelf, or in a computer. He needs to be treasured within your heart. This is all accomplished through faith, and this faith roots you and grounds you in love in Him for eternity. You are now able to see the four dimensions of love in your three dimensional existence. You are told love is deep, high, long, and wide. Do you believe this? Do you appropriate this truth to those who are difficult and tough to love? This is why love is so hard to figure out. For instance, why does God love you so much? Were you worth it before He saved you and redeemed you? How much does He get in return for His buck? Not much bang, is there? Yet, He found it worth everything to purchase you and to see you learning this. You are in Him now; therefore, you are priceless to the Father of heaven! This is why it is unknowable. You will never figure out why He loves you so much, even though you will spend eternity with Him because of it.

Lastly, Paul writes you are filled with all the fullness of God. He is fully within you, as well as everywhere at the same time. You are completely in Him and He is completely in you. Now it's easy for you to consider your being in Him when you think of His omnipresence, but it twists and stretches your mind a little to think of His being completely inside of you, let alone fully dwelling within your heart.

## The Apostles' Prayer

**Matthew 6:5-13** *"And when you pray, you shall not be like the hypocrites. For they love to pray standing in the synagogues and on the corners of the streets, that they may be seen by men. Assuredly, I say to you, they have their reward. But you, when you pray, go into your room, and when you have shut your door, pray to your Father who is in the secret place; and your Father who sees in secret will reward you openly. And when you pray, do not use vain repetitions as the heathen do. For they think that they will be heard for their many words. Therefore do not be like them. For your Father knows the things you have need of before you ask Him. In this manner, therefore, pray: Our Father in heaven, hallowed be Your name. Your kingdom come. Your will be done on earth as it is in heaven. Give us this day our daily bread. And forgive us our debts, as we forgive our debtors. And do not lead us into temptation, but deliver us from the evil one. For Yours is the kingdom and the power and the glory forever. Amen."*

Jesus gave this example of prayer to the Apostles when they asked Him how they should pray. It is often referred to as the LORD's Prayer, but it is more accurately identified as the Apostles' Prayer. The opening clause of the Apostles' Prayer demonstrates for you your needed adoration of the Father. In the middle section of this prayer, you see your need for your confession of sin. The prayer closes with an attitude of thanksgiving and adoration.

Jesus began by telling them their prayers should not be like the hypocrites and should not cause all the attention to be brought upon the person praying. He addresses the religious here and reveals the focus of their hearts. This is all done for the praise of men, not the praise of God. These men are more mindful of men than of God. Jesus states if there are only men to hear you and if that is who is important to you, then that is all the reward you will get. The praise of men doesn't last long, and it isn't very satisfying or fulfilling.

God, on the other hand, sees where no man can see and that is in the inner rooms of the heart. He tells you that you should not worry about your rewards or your praise. God is a faithful rewarder. He is just and He never forgets the wages earned, whether it be for good or evil. He states your reward will be seen in the open and revealed to all who are present with Him, that is—all the saints. **2 Corinthians 5:10**, *"For we must all appear before the judgment seat of Christ, that each one may receive the things done in the body, according to what he has done, whether good or bad."* On a side note, this reward is all that will be seen because everything else is wiped away by the precious blood of the Lamb. You don't have to worry about a public screening of all your sins. You will stand before the BEMA seat, the seat of rewards, not the seat of CONDEMNATION or JUDGMENT. (Hebrews 11:6; 1 Corinthians 3:11-15)

Jesus tells you not to use vain words or many words. Vain words usually have to do with flattery and pride. The Bible doesn't have much good to say about them. The Bible also tells you that in many words sin is not lacking (Proverbs 10:19). Jesus then tells them not to imitate the hypocrites, because your heavenly Father knows your needs before you do. You can trust Him fully and completely.

Jesus then begins to show you how to pray. You'll notice He is speaking to His own children, which means a person has to know Him personally, not just as a god. This is a model of prayer you are to repeat both in public and in private. It illustrates four important matters in presentation: 1) your <u>attitudes</u> in which you should approach God, 2) an <u>order</u> which you, as God's child, should take when you make your requests known to Him, 3) the priority of your needs (<u>a correct focus</u>), and 4) the <u>adoration</u> which is due your Father in heaven when you make your supplications known.

You find the example of this prayer in the Gospel of Matthew, as well as the Gospel of Luke. This model is for both Jews (Matthew was written from a Jewish perspective) and Gentiles (Luke addresses Jesus from a Gentile perspective). It is for everyone and everybody.

Notice Jesus has your focus on others, not on self. This is indicated by the words "us" and "our," as opposed to "me" or "my." The focus of the Apostles' Prayer is on God and others, not so much on you. The first three portions of this prayer show your heart must be right before Him; they are concerned about your relationship with Him. It shows that God and others are to be your first and foremost concern. The needs of self are to be secondary. The last four petitions are concerned with your own welfare and needs. It also shows this prayer has to be of the heart, not just of the lips.

The Apostle's Prayer states God is in heaven. How far does your voice normally travel? Across the room? Across the field? Across the canyon? To the clouds? If your voice that is uttered by your lips cannot be heard far on the earth, how can you expect God to hear you in the throne room of heaven? The only voice God can and will hear is that of a broken and contrite heart, one who is contrite and poor in spirit. (Isaiah 66:2; Psalms 34:18, 51:17; Philippians 2:3-4)

## "Our Father in heaven"

In the first stanza of this prayer, you are introduced to the importance of whom you are addressing. You must have a personal and living relationship with the God of heaven before you can address Him as your Father. This relationship must be secured through the acceptance of the sacrifice of God's one and only Son, Jesus Christ. The new covenant was purchased through the blood of Christ. The phrase "Our Father in heaven" means these following four things.

He is the God of love. **1 John 4:16**, *"And we have known and believed the love that God has for us. God is love, and he who abides in love abides in God, and God in him."*

He is the God, your Father, who created you. **Malachi 2:10**, *"Have we not all one Father? Has not one God created us? Why do we deal treacherously with one another by profaning the covenant of the fathers?"*

He is your Father by covenant because of Jesus, His Son. **Hebrews 13:20-21**, *"Now may the God of peace who brought up our Lord Jesus from the dead, that great Shepherd of the sheep, through the blood of the everlasting covenant, make you complete in every good work to do His will, working in you what is well pleasing in His sight, through Jesus Christ, to whom be glory forever and ever. Amen."*

He grants you His divine nature to operate in this world. This is granted because of this covenant, by virtue of partaking of Christ and accepting His free gift of grace. **Galatians 4:6**, *"And because you are sons, God has sent forth the Spirit of His Son into your hearts, crying out, 'Abba, Father!'"* **2 Peter 1:3-4**, *"… as His divine power has given to us all things that pertain to life and godliness, through the knowledge of Him who called us by glory and virtue, by which have been given to us exceedingly great and precious promises, that through these you may be partakers of the divine nature, having escaped the corruption that is in the world through lust."*

## "Your kingdom come"

If you ask for His kingdom to come, you acknowledge you are not in it or a part of it as long as you are here on earth. You ask Him to lovingly enable you to perform His will, not your own. You ask Him to perform His will through you the same way it is done in the kingdom in heaven, and you acknowledge His will is better than your own.

Prayer is the wrestling arena where you exercise, bruise, and bring into submission your will. Your will is the most stubborn and rebellious of all the components of your being. Have you ever noticed how hard it is to just settle down and rest before the LORD when in prayer? Is it hard for you to just stop and listen for His voice? Is it hard for you to be calm and to quiet those inner voices in your soul? Do you have a quiet time or quiet place to retreat to when you want to get alone with God? If not, you should.

Your will plays a major part with all these components. If you don't spend time practicing your surrender to His will and resting in His holy presence, you will truly find it very difficult to pray when you really need to. Prayer is often thought of as being a one-way conversation. It is not. Prayer allows you to commune and fellowship with your Creator. It allows you to gain insight into His wisdom and plan for your life. Prayer allows you to find the pathway to walk on as you travel through this world. It helps you to keep your armor on and your loads of life light. Remember, His yoke is easy and His burden is light.

## "our daily bread"

Next, you ask God to provide your daily bread. Your earthly needs are supplied by the kindness of your heavenly Father.

## "forgive us"

This verse teaches your past sins have been forgiven and you should pray fervently for grace so you are prevented from repeating the same sins again. Grace teaches you not to sin. <u>You cannot ask for forgiveness from God unless you truly desire to abstain from sin.</u>

Forgiveness is not a turnstile. You cannot continue in your sin as though you were just going in circles. An example of this could be, "Please forgive me," and then keep going in the same circle, repeating the same pattern, practice, or habit…and then asking again, "Please forgive me, please forgive me."

In order to receive forgiveness you must <u>repent</u> (stop, turn around, or do a 180-degree turn and go the opposite direction). Grace enables you to come to your senses. You truly begin to understand your freedom in Christ. Because of this revelation, you begin to be repulsed by the practice of the sins in your life. You begin to mourn over them and the consequences that transpire in the lives of others, as well as your own. You ask for the guilt and shame caused by the sin to be removed from you. It is here you ask for His holy power to be working in you and the ability to walk in that deliverance.

"Our sins are forgiven through the mediation of the Son and you are preserved from temptation and delivered from evil by the gracious operations of the Holy Spirit." (*Arthur W. Pink, An Exposition of the Sermon on the Mount, Baker Book House, 1975*)

## "do not lead us into temptation"

Here you ask a strange petition. You ask God not to lead you into temptation. What is meant by this request? You are told in the scriptures God cannot tempt anyone with evil. **James 1:13**, "*Let no one say when he is tempted, 'I am tempted by God'; for God cannot be tempted by evil, nor does He Himself tempt anyone.*"

So why would Jesus place in the closing portion of this model prayer a petition to not lead into temptation? Let's take a closer look so you can understand and teach others.

**Temptation:** The first and primary meaning of the word tempt is to make trial of a person in order to find out what is truly in him, what he is made of, and what he will do. It brings out your true focus. Your focus affects six things: your direction, your devotion, and your desires, as well as your worship, your walk, and your works. All of these six things are independent, as well as intimately related.

The meaning of the phrase "God tempts no man" is that He neither introduces nor inspires evil to come into your heart, nor can He cause anyone to perform evil. He cannot in any way be a partner with you in your guilt. You are completely responsible yourself. You can't blame anyone else for your sin. It is manifested by your will practicing lawlessness. **James 1:14-15**, *"But each one is tempted when he is drawn away by his own desires and enticed. Then, when desire has conceived, it gives birth to sin; and sin, when it is full-grown, brings forth death."* You seek anything to blame but yourself including blaming the temptations you find yourself looking into and falling prey to. If that doesn't work, you blame God Himself for your fall because of His goodness to you.

**Genesis 22:1** *Now it came to pass after these things that God tested Abraham, and said to him, "Abraham!" And he said, "Here I am."*

God, on the other hand, <u>does</u> test your fortitude and integrity. This test brought Abraham closer to God by faith. He believed God and therefore was willing to do anything for Him. This faith was not blind, and this test only reaffirmed the trust Abraham had in God. God tested Abraham's faith and fidelity.

**Test:** *To test, try, prove, assay, put to the proof or test* (OLB).

Contrary to this type of testing is temptation. This is done by Satan himself or his minions. In Satan's temptation of Christ, you see he sought to bring down His morality, which was impossible to do. It was the exact same model of temptation he successfully used on Adam. Remember <u>Adam was created morally innocent, not perfect.</u>

**Matthew 5:45** *"...that you may be sons of your Father in heaven; for He makes His sun rise on the evil and on the good, and sends rain on the just and on the unjust."*

So again, what does it mean "lead us not into temptation" if God cannot tempt you? Throughout the scriptures, you see God's universal providence is owned by Him and made abundantly clear. The following scriptures show God is in control over all things, including evil and temptation. Read them and write down what speaks to you and what you learn from them. (Psalms 104 and 145; Acts 17:25-28; Isaiah 45:6-7; Isaiah 40:12-14)

**1 Corinthians 10:13** *No temptation has overtaken you except such as is common to man; but God is faithful, who will not allow you to be tempted beyond what you are able, but with the temptation will also make the way of escape, that you may be able to bear it.*

God has the same control over evil as He does over good.

**Romans 5:6-10** *For when we were still without strength, in due time Christ died for the ungodly. For scarcely for a righteous man will one die; yet perhaps for a good man someone would even dare to die. But God demonstrates His own love toward us, in that while we were still sinners, Christ died for us. Much more then, having now been justified by His blood, we shall be saved from wrath through Him. For if when we were enemies we were reconciled to God through the death of His Son, much more, having been reconciled, we shall be saved by His life.*

In your unregenerate and fallen state, you deserve to be completely devoured by evil. The truth is God would be just in allowing this to happen. He is not and never has been obligated to save you. However, to the praise of His glorious grace He did and that by His own choice. Truly, this kind of love is a mystery. Your mercy is recognized upon the moment of your reconciliation with your Maker and His forgiveness of your sins. (Romans 2:4; 1 John 2:1-2; 2 Corinthians 5:21)

You are totally unable to overcome your intrinsic state of being and your weakness is acknowledged. You, on your own, are not able to stand up to temptations. You give in every time. The lust that lies within you is too active and powerful to overcome without the help of your Savior.

What causes you to think God leads you into temptation? Sometimes God sees fit that you should be tempted objectively through His divine providence or provision, which though good in themselves, offer occasions within you to be tempted to sin. If and when these occasions arise, you ask that you may not yield to them, or if you yield, that you may not be absolutely overcome by them. The things that make you vulnerable to these occasions are self-righteousness, self-reliance, self-confidence, and complacency.

**Luke 22:31-32** *And the Lord said, "Simon, Simon! Indeed, Satan has asked for you, that he may sift you as wheat. But I have prayed for you, that your faith should not fail; and when you have returned to Me, strengthen your brethren."*

This example illustrates God sometimes permits Satan to tempt you. God does this not only to show you what is within you, but also to show Satan the perfect work of grace is able to withstand all he can throw at you. When God does not restrain Satan (and He is under no obligation to do so), you are sometimes seen as wheat on the threshing floor. (Job 1:8; 2:3)

**1 Corinthians 5:4-5** *In the name of our Lord Jesus Christ, when you are gathered together, along with my spirit, with the power of our Lord Jesus Christ, deliver such a one to Satan for the destruction of the flesh, that his spirit may be saved in the day of the Lord Jesus.*

Sometimes God allows Satan to chasten you in order to change your course or direction. This is shown by having the devil rule and reign over the unrepentant sinner or backslider in heart, allowing the devil to lead the sinner into further sin because of his stubbornness and rebellion. God allows this to happen in order to drive you back to Him or to Him for the first time, to humble you, and to glorify Himself by manifesting more fully to you His ability to preserve you by His power, mercy, and grace. (2 Timothy 2:25-26; Jude 22-23; 2 Peter 2:12-13)

Now the obvious question arises—why are you tested?

First, He tries you or tests you in order to reveal to you your weakness and your deep need of His grace. **2 Chronicles 32:31**, *"However, regarding the ambassadors of the princes of Babylon, whom they sent to him to inquire about the wonder that was done in the land, God withdrew from him, in order to test him, that He might know all that was in his heart."*

Second, He allows the testing because of your need to recognize your need of Him. **Psalms 119:117**, *"Hold me up, and I shall be safe, and I shall observe Your statutes continually."*

Third, God allows you to be tested in order to teach you your need to be watchful and prayerful. **Luke 21:34-36**, *"But take heed to yourselves, lest your hearts be weighed down with carousing, drunkenness, and cares of this life, and that Day come on you unexpectedly. For it will come as a snare on all those who dwell on the face of the whole earth. Watch therefore, and pray always that you may be counted worthy to escape all these things that will come to pass, and to stand before the Son of Man."* **Luke 22:40**, *"When He came to the place, He said to them, 'Pray that you may not enter into temptation.'"*

Fourth, God allows you to be tested in order to cure laziness. You, because of God's goodness, sometimes fall prey to complacency or take for granted His wonderful provision. You then, as the scriptures state, fall asleep in the light. **Ephesians 5:14**, *"Therefore He says: 'Awake, you who sleep, arise from the dead, and Christ will give you light.'"*

Last, God allows you to be tested to show you the importance of the armor of God, that your enemies are <u>never flesh and blood</u> but instead are the rulers of this world. Remember this world is under the dominion of the devil. **Ephesians 6:11-18**, *"Put on the whole armor of God, that you may be able to stand against the wiles of the devil. For we do not wrestle against flesh and blood, but against principalities, against powers, against the rulers of the darkness of this age, against spiritual hosts of wickedness in the heavenly places. Therefore take up the whole armor of God, that you may be able to withstand in the evil day, and having done all, to stand. Stand therefore, having girded your waist with truth, having put on the breastplate of righteousness, and having shod your feet with the preparation of the gospel of peace; above all, taking the shield of faith with which you will be able to quench all the fiery darts of the wicked one. And take the helmet of salvation, and the sword of the Spirit, which is the word of God; praying always with all prayer and supplication in the Spirit, being watchful to this end with all perseverance and supplication for all the saints..."*

**Hebrews 2:10, 17-18; 4:15** *For it was fitting for Him, for whom are all things and by whom are all things, in bringing many sons to glory, to make the captain of their salvation perfect through sufferings. ... Therefore, in all things He had to be made like His brethren, that He might be a merciful and faithful High Priest in things pertaining to God, to make propitiation for the sins of the people. For in that He Himself has suffered, being tempted, He is able to aid those who are tempted. ...For we do not have a High Priest who cannot sympathize with our weaknesses, but was in all points tempted as we are, yet without sin.*

These verses show to be tempted or temptations themselves are not sin and not all temptations are evil. Sin is what results from what you do with temptations and the outcome when you yield to them. Jesus was tempted but He never gave in to sin. Since Jesus was tempted, temptations are not sin. Notice God, the Holy Spirit, drove Jesus into the wilderness to be tempted. Sometimes God puts you to the test. In this case, He put His own Son to the test so you could have a pathway to follow and be led on to be delivered. (Matthew 4:1; Mark 1:12-13)

**James 1:2-4** *My brethren, count it all joy when you fall into various trials, knowing that the testing of your faith produces patience. But let patience have its perfect work, that you may be perfect and complete, lacking nothing.*

When you fall into temptations, you pray and ask for release from the judgments of these sins and the ability through grace to repent of these sins.

**Psalms 19:13** *Keep back Your servant also from presumptuous sins; let them not have dominion over me. Then I shall be blameless, and I shall be innocent of great transgression.*

Finally, you have a responsibility to avoid the people, places, and things that would lead you back to these temptations. You must steadfastly resist the devil. You submissively and willingly go to God for grace for the ability to resist familiarity and the devil. The measure God grants you is according to His own good pleasure. (Proverbs 4:14-15; James 4:7-8; Song of Solomon 2:15; 1 Thessalonians 5:22; Philippians 2:13)

## "deliver us from evil"

The last phrases listed in this prayer show you the need to be delivered from the evil one. Here are four examples of the wonderful grace of God. They are a <u>providing grace</u> illustrated by the phrase "give us," a <u>pardoning grace</u> illustrated by the phrase "forgive us," a <u>preventing grace</u> illustrated by the phrase "lead us," and lastly, a <u>preserving grace</u> illustrated by the phrase "deliver us."

When you pray, you are to pray you would be delivered from Satan, as well as sin itself, the world, and your own corrupt nature. Again, please note you are not praying just for yourself but for the whole body, and this is signified by the word "us."

**1 John 3:3** *And everyone who has this hope in Him purifies himself, just as He is pure.*

**Galatians 1:4** *...who gave Himself for our sins, that He might deliver us from this present evil age, according to the will of our God and Father,...*

These two verses show God has answered His model prayer for you because His purifying love enables you to be true. He provided deliverance from the evil one through Christ His Son. (Romans 12:9; Matthew 12:35)

**Romans 6:6, 18** *...knowing this, that our old man was crucified with Him, that the body of sin might be done away with, that we should no longer be slaves of sin.... And having been set free from sin, you became slaves of righteousness.*

As a child of God, you have been translated into the kingdom of Christ and light. Therefore, Satan no longer has authority or dominion over you now because you have been set free from sin. (Colossians 1:12-13; Romans 6:14)

Jesus himself prayed you would not be overcome by sin or the evil one and you would become one with Him (John 17:20-22). **John 17:15**, *"I do not pray that You should take them out of the world, but that You should keep them from the evil one."*

## "yours is the kingdom"

Finally, you come to the doxology: *"For Yours is the kingdom and the power and the glory forever. Amen."* This powerful phrase completes this prayer and reflects the glory that God alone deserves the worship, credit, and praise.

**Psalms 67:5-6** *Let the peoples praise You, O God; let all the peoples praise You. Then the earth shall yield her increase; God, our own God, shall bless us.*

**Colossians 4:2** *Continue earnestly in prayer, being vigilant in it with thanksgiving…*

It is important to give God praise, thanks, and adoration. You are to bring all things to God, be humble, and give Him praise and adoration for His everlasting mercy. The Apostle's Prayer shows you have been chosen from before time and His love for you was from everlasting to everlasting. (Philippians 4:6; 1 Peter 5:6-7; Ephesians 1:11; Jeremiah 31:3)

**Hebrews 13:8** *Jesus Christ is the same yesterday, today, and forever.*

Isn't it comforting to know He whom you petition never changes and is all-powerful? God is for you—who can be against you (Romans 8:31)! There is nothing impossible for Him. Doesn't that prove He deserves everything you can give to Him? (Psalms 90:2; Romans 8:31; Jeremiah 32:17, 27)

## "Amen"

Jesus closes this prayer with the simple word amen, which simply means so be it. Remember if the Bible says it, you believe it, and that settles it! As you can see from the examples listed here in the model prayer the LORD gave you, you have an incredible blessing in your ability to communicate and fellowship with a perfect and holy Creator. He was never obligated to hear or listen to you, and He certainly was never held in bondage to save you. You will never be able to claim you are the cause or the treasure that caused Him to save you, and you can never take credit for putting that into His mind. God saved you according to His own will and love for you. Oh, how great is this love!

# Questions for Lesson 7

1. What is the standard of conduct laid out for you to take heed of in Proverbs 4:20-22?

2. What is one of the most pleasing things God loves His children to say back to Him?

3. Where does Paul's and your strength come from, where does it need to be focused?

4. When saying the Apostles' Prayer, why should you not draw attention to yourself or allow this prayer to be stated in a hypocritical way or as a talisman or charm?

5. Why are you told not to worry about your rewards that will be given by God to you? Why is this so different from what you worry about here on earth?

6. What four items are illustrated for you in the Apostles' Prayer?

7. In your own words, describe what these four items do for your prayer life and what they remind you of.

8. What is the focus of the Apostles' Prayer?

9. What is the only voice God can and will hear, and why won't God hear someone who is proud in heart? Look at Isaiah 66:2. How does James 4:6 fit into God hearing you?

10. What are the four things the statement "Our Father in heaven" means?

11. What are you asking God to do when you are asking for His kingdom to come?

12. What is accomplished in the wrestling arena of prayer? Why is this important?

13. Why is the phrase "Forgive us" so important to you? What is the underlying meaning according to your lesson? What teaches you to turn from your sins?

14. What is the difference between testing and temptation?

15. Why does God allow Satan to chasten you?

16. What are the five reasons for God testing you?

17. What is your responsibility when it comes to temptations?

18. What are the four examples of grace of God in this wonderful prayer?

19. What does the final doxology show you?

# A New Life in Jesus

I remember my first experience with alcohol. When I was 11, I stayed with relatives in Florida for the summer. One of them handed me a beer and said, "Here, have a drink." When I said, "No, thanks," he refused to take it back and said, "I'm going to make a man out of you." By the time I got to high school, I thought the way to be a man was to drink and do drugs with everyone else.

In 1983, one of my best friends died suddenly at 17 in a freak accident; he was struck by lightening. After that, I started to think more about heaven and hell and where I would spend eternity. I knew there was a God because of the way I was raised, but I did not want to be some kind of Jesus freak. That would have made me an outsider with my friends. So, I thought if I could prove the Bible was right about Satan and hell, it must be right about Jesus and heaven.

I started to try to find hell by using drugs. One day while I was smoking with my brothers, my world started to spin and I felt like I was going to pass out. When I sat down, I felt like my soul was falling from me and it was like I was utterly alone. It was so horrifying I cannot put it into words, but it must be what hell is like—total separation from God. I knew I didn't want any part of that. Shortly after that, I quit doing drugs but kept drinking heavily.

As far as I was concerned, my life was pretty messed up. I just wanted it to end; I wasn't sure if I really wanted to die, but I couldn't go on the way I was. I wanted a chance at a new life. Because of my vision of hell, I didn't want to go there. But I thought if I killed myself, I would go to hell (that's what I was taught as a child at church). I thought I would go to heaven if God took my life for me, so I started praying that God would let me be run over by a truck or something.

My brother who was saved invited me to a church service with him. At first I said no, but later I went back and said, "Yes, I'll go. I don't understand it, but something tells me when I go I'll find what I am looking for there, and it will drive me crazy until I check it out." When the speaker asked if anyone wanted to have a new life in Jesus, I jumped up and ran forward.

I became a new person that night and started to make some changes. When I got home that night, I did something some people have never understood (My dad still brings it up sometimes. He doesn't know why I did it, but he knows there was a change in me from that point forward.). I broke all of my bottles of alcohol I had been saving and reusing. I must have been funny to watch—I would break one and sweep it up, break another one, and sweep it up. To me, it was an outward sign of my inner commitment not to drink and to follow Jesus.

I have been following Him ever since and have never regretted my choice.

Fuzzy

# Lesson 8: The Importance of Serving, Principle 12

As you begin this overview of Principle 12, you have the tremendous blessing and ability to take a moment to see the faithfulness of God during your journey. By now, you have observed and experienced the changes that have transpired within your heart and life. These changes were at first imperceptible from your vantage point, but with the encouragement and exhortation from your fellow brothers and sisters in the LORD, you began to see the truth of this transformation.

The final phase of this transformation is serving. There are four items that verify the supernatural change of your heart and character. These are (1) the ability to humble yourself before God, (2) the desire to be fully dependent upon Him, (3) the ability to accept help from others, and finally, (4) the ability to deny yourself and be a servant to others.

Observe the ecosystem of a lake. A lake has both an inlet and an outlet, whereas a pond has only an inlet. Lakes are kept fresh and alive because of current and waves. Waves come in, lap upon the shore, and produce oxygen in the water. An outlet creates a current which helps regulate the temperature and keeps the circulation of the oxygen fresh and full. In contrast, a pond can also have waves but it becomes stale and infested with algae because there is no outlet. The algae absorb all the oxygen suffocating the life in the pond. Algae live on carbon dioxide produced by the warm water and the decomposing life within the pond. This decomposition process takes place because there isn't an outlet to complete the circulatory system (which regulates the temperature and keeps the water fresh).

When you serve others, you allow the supernatural circulatory system to work. This is seen in the process of receiving and giving. God is the giver of every good and perfect gift. The more you give to others, the more you receive from Him. The more you receive from Him, the more you desire to give in His name. The more grace is revealed and acknowledged from the heart, the more outpouring of gratitude will flow from it. The more gratitude you have, the more you will desire and be enabled to give. The more you give, the more maturity in Christ is manifested and observed and the more you will receive from God to give to others.

The more you are changed into the image of Christ, the more you will be aware of your sins. The more you are made aware of your sins, the less you will be apt to lean upon yourself. The less you lean upon yourself, the more humble you will become. The more humble you are made to be, the more God will lift you up. Scripture makes it very clear the longer you abide in Christ, the more the desire will grow within you to be made like Him. This is the direct result of the manifestation of grace within your life.

The order of your new priority list in Christ reads like this—Jesus first, others second, and self last. This is a change only God can reveal and manifest within you, and it takes Him to change your narcissistic ways. Only by being a Spirit-filled child of God are you enabled to overcome your self-centeredness and the action it causes which is selfishness. This is a daily battle for the Christian, new or old, and <u>it lasts for a lifetime</u>.

With these things in mind, turn your attention to the final principle. Before you start, please pray to the Lord to open your heart to reveal His truths for you. These truths are necessary to give you vision, hope, desire, and life to move through trials and tribulations that you will be confronted with in life.

**Principle 12 - *HAVING BEEN ACTIVELY LIVING OUT THESE PRINCIPLES AND SEEING THE FRUIT OF RECONCILIATION AND RESTORATION IN MY LIFE, I NOW DESIRE TO FULFILL THE COMMAND OF CHRIST, TO SHARE HIM WITH THOSE WHO ARE STILL CAUGHT IN A LIFESTYLE WHICH SUBJECTS THEM TO THE BONDAGE OF SIN AND FEAR, AND TO PRACTICE THE LORD'S PRINCIPLES IN ALL AREAS OF MY LIFE.***

The first part of Principle 12 is a personal experience of the spiritual regeneration that happened when you received and accepted Jesus Christ into your life. By His grace and free gift, you became born again and came into a right relationship with God the Father. You then were filled with the Holy Spirit who has empowered and allowed you to fulfill and live out your heavenly Father's will. (Romans 8:9-11; Colossians 2:9-10).

The second part was experienced when you came to the revelation revealed in **Matthew 10:8**, "*Freely you have received, freely give.*" You will never grow in maturity nor can you keep what you will not give away if you don't heed the principle stated in **Luke 9:24**, "*For whoever desires to save his life will lose it, but whoever loses his life for My sake will save it.*"

If having Jesus in your life is the greatest thing that has ever happened to you, nothing should keep you from telling others about Him. At a minimum, you will be compelled to serve others and let them see Him through your actions and service to them; He is alive and well within your heart and life.

Finally, the practice of all the Lord's principles causes an ongoing, one-day-at-a-time, way of living in which you will continue to grow in the Lord and be renewed and transformed daily from faith to faith and glory to glory. This does not mean you cannot plan your life.

**2 Corinthians 1:3-4** *Blessed be the God and Father of our Lord Jesus Christ, the Father of mercies and God of all comfort, who comforts us in all our tribulation, that we may be able to comfort those who are in any trouble, with the comfort with which we ourselves are comforted by God.*

You offer your adoration and obeisance to your Father and to your LORD. You address them both as blessed and make joyful thanks to bestow blessing and praise upon them. This wonderful letter opens with praise, and all of it goes to the Father and Lord of all. Praise also goes to the Savior who has given you eternal life and restored your fellowship and communion with Him.

This verse states God is the Father of mercies. He was the original giver of this awesome gift. Mercy always follows grace, and both are by-products of love. Mercy means to pity or have compassion on someone. When you think of pity you usually think of being looked down upon because you found yourself in need. Pity usually leaves a bad taste in your mouth because of your knowledge and experience in the secular realm. In fact, in many cases you were repulsed, offended, and stumbled by the lack of caring and response to your need.

God's pity is different from the world's. God sees the needs of His children and goes beyond the need. The scriptures define pity as to love, love deeply, have mercy, be compassionate, have tender affection, and to have compassion upon. When God pities someone, He not only ministers to the need but also lavishes more supplies upon the need than is really necessary. A good example of this is found in John 3:16. You didn't want a Savior but your heavenly Father knew you needed Him to save you from your sin, so He sent His only Son to die in your place. By doing this, you, who were poor, became rich in Christ. He gave you more than you would ever need or could imagine and in the process—He solved the unknown and unrecognized problem all mankind suffered from—separation from God. (Ephesians 2:13)

God also is the God of all comfort. Comfort means *consolation, a calling near, summons* (OLB). When you call out for comfort, God will come alongside you to bring you consolation. You gain comfort and consolation because you call out to Him. You draw near to God, and when you draw near to Him, He draws near to you.

When you are in tribulation, you cry out for God to come near you and He does. Tribulation means *a pressing, pressing together, pressure;* metaphorically: *oppression, affliction, distress, straits* (OLB). You are told in Romans 12:2 the world desires to press you into its mold. The world is always applying pressure upon you. **2 Corinthians 4:7-9**, "*But we have this treasure in earthen vessels, that the excellence of the power may be of God and not of us. We are hard-pressed on every side, yet not crushed; we are perplexed, but not in despair; persecuted, but not forsaken; struck down, but not destroyed …*"

Because you have received this comfort from God, you are now able to comfort others because of the new life in you. You have a desire to come alongside others in similar situations who cry out, and you respond by coming alongside them. The love of Christ compels you (from the KJ "constraineth"), which means *to hold together with constraint, to compress, to press on every side* (OLB). When the world tries to tear you apart or crush you, God, who indwells you, keeps you together. He presses out all the dents the world perpetrates against you as you go against the flow of the world. He balances the pressures that are in constant play in the environment of this world.

Serving is one way of bringing comfort to another person in times of tribulation or suffering. You are able to meet the need with the same comfort you received from your own experiences. This keeps both of you from focusing on self and helps them avoid the snare of self-pity.

**Galatians 6:1-4** *Brethren, if a man is overtaken in any trespass, you who are spiritual restore such a one in a spirit of gentleness, considering yourself lest you also be tempted. 2 Bear one another's burdens, and so fulfill the law of Christ. 3 For if anyone thinks himself to be something, when he is nothing, he deceives himself. 4 But let each one examine his own work, and then he will have rejoicing in himself alone, and not in another.*

One of the temptations you face when you come across someone who is suffering is to judge them as though they were responsible for their plight. Not all suffering is self-inflicted. In verse 1, you see a man who is overtaken in a sin and it doesn't matter whether or not it is his fault; your instructions are to be gentle with him. You understand your desire to help is caused by your spirituality in Christ. You are governed by the Holy Spirit, not the spirit of the world. Therefore, you are equipped to meet whatever need there is.

The idea here is this person is taken by surprise and overcome by sin. When you come alongside a person like this, you are to restore them (*to mend (what has been broken or rent), to repair, to complete. Ethically: to strengthen, perfect, complete, make one what he ought to be* (OLB)). You are to restore the person in the spirit of meekness (*gentleness, mildness* (OLB)). Gentleness or meekness is the opposite of self-assertiveness and self-esteem. Meekness stems from trust in God's goodness and His control over the situation. The gentle person is not occupied with self at all. This is a work of the Holy Spirit, not of the human will.

The word considering means consider your own weakness and susceptibility to temptation before you deal severely with the erring brother, and then you are to restore him in view of that fact. God enables you to do this now because you have a centered, balanced perspective of yourself given by and through the Holy Spirit. You now know who you are without pretense. God has revealed your flaws, as well as given you the solutions to bind up your wounds and heal. This verse cautions you to be careful because you can be tempted to judge rather than to serve the hurting individual.

The word tempted means the possibility of falling into the temptation to sin when you try to restore an erring brother. The correct way to restore another is to do so without the desire to act as his judge. You realize it is possible for you to fall to the same sin or find yourself in similar circumstances. (1 Corinthians 4:5)

On the positive side, tempted means *to try, make trial of, test: for the purpose of ascertaining his quantity, or what he thinks, or how he will behave himself.* On the negative side it means *to test one maliciously, craftily to put to the proof his feelings or judgments (OLB).*

Galatians 6:2 tells you to bear one another's burdens, come alongside each other when you discern your fellow brethren are struggling with the same things you have struggled with. You are to comfort them by coming alongside them, by listening to them and assisting them—without enabling them. Enabling is easing the pain level because of a lack of understanding of God's purposes of discipline or your own selfish ambitions. You are not to allow them to ignore or escape the responsibility and consequences of their actions but you are to help them by pointing out their options. Jesus, in His mercy, will deal with the consequences.

The last part of verse 2 tells you what you are doing when you bear another's burdens—you are fulfilling the law of Christ. This means love your neighbor as much as you already love yourself. Jesus told you He was giving you a new commandment "to love one another; as I have loved you, that you also love one another." You can see the meaning of your Lord's words in the Sermon on the Mount, **Matthew 7:1, 5, 12**, *"Judge not, that you be not judged…. Hypocrite! First remove the plank from your own eye, and then you will see clearly to remove the speck from your brother's eye…. Therefore, whatever you want men to do to you, do also to them, for this is the Law and the Prophets."*

In verse 3 of Galatians 6, you are cautioned not to think too highly of yourself. This is the number one temptation you face as sponsors, disciplers, or teachers. You can have the tendency of placing yourself on a higher level than those with whom you are working. (Romans 2:1)

In verse 4, you are humbled by what you read, that is, in truth you are nothing. Scripture points out your sufficiency comes from Christ alone. **2 Corinthians 3:5**, *"Not that we are sufficient of ourselves to think of anything as being from ourselves, but our sufficiency is from God."* If you are not plugged into the Lord and His resources, you are totally insufficient for any job that comes your way. Jesus put it this way when He stated in **John 15:5**, *"I am the vine, you are the branches. He who abides in Me, and I in him, bears much fruit; for without Me you can do nothing."*

**Matthew 9:35-38** *Then Jesus went about all the cities and villages, teaching in their synagogues, preaching the gospel of the kingdom, and healing every sickness and every disease among the people. But when He saw the multitudes, He was moved with compassion for them, because they were weary and scattered, like sheep having no shepherd. Then He said to His disciples, "The harvest truly is plentiful, but the laborers are few. Therefore pray the Lord of the harvest to send out laborers into His harvest."*

In these verses, you see the Lord's heart as He went about the cities and villages. God always makes His message known to all people. His desire is for all of mankind to be saved so He makes sure everybody has a chance to know and accept Him. You'll also notice He went about preaching first to the Jews in the synagogues and then to the Gentiles in the streets. He preached the gospel of the kingdom and then to prove what He was stating was true, He healed those who had diseases of every kind.

God's compassion can be seen by His identification with your afflictions. Because He came in the form of man, He can sympathize with your weaknesses (Hebrews 2:17). Jesus identified your two most prolific issues. One is your weakness and inability to save yourself because you are without strength (Romans 5:6). Paul states in **Romans 7:18**, *"For I know that in me (that is, in my flesh) nothing good dwells; for to will is present with me, but how to perform what is good I do not find."* The second weakness common to all mankind is his inability to find his own way to God. You are *"like sheep having no shepherd,"* and you are truly scattered. Scripture points out the truth about you. **Jeremiah 10:23**, *"O LORD, I know the way of man is not in himself; it is not in man who walks to direct his own steps."* **Proverbs 20:24**, *"A man's steps are of the LORD; how then can a man understand his own way?"* **1 Peter 2:25a**, *"For you were like sheep going astray ..."*

**1 Corinthians 9:19-23** *For though I am free from all men, I have made myself a servant to all, that I might win the more; 20 and to the Jews I became as a Jew, that I might win Jews; to those who are under the law, as under the law, that I might win those who are under the law; 21 to those who are without law, as without law (not being without law toward God, but under law toward Christ), that I might win those who are without law; 22 to the weak I became as weak, that I might win the weak. I have become all things to all men, that I might by all means save some. 23 Now this I do for the gospel's sake, that I may be partaker of it with you.*

In these verses, you see the essence of Principle 12. <u>You are free to live for yourself and to do what you want but the spiritual change that has developed in you causes you to desire to serve your fellow man.</u> **2 Corinthians 5:14-15**, *"For the love of Christ compels us, because we judge thus: that if One died for all, then all died; and He died for all, that those who live should live no longer for themselves, but for*

*Him who died for them and rose again.*" The love that lives within you compels you to love others. It is a direct result of having the nature and character of Christ dwelling within you. The scripture points out you are free but your perspective has been changed. Now you see the value of giving yourself away and how it provides more dividends than you could ever hold. **Luke 9:24**, *"For whoever desires to save his life will lose it, but whoever loses his life for My sake will save it."* Thus, you see the meaning of the end of verse 19, *"that I might win the more."*

Verses 20 through 22 show this change is not based on hypocrisy. It is a real change all those you serve can know for certain you are real with them. The desire for all to hear the message of the Gospel and see the truth that will set them free causes a zeal within you that supersedes your selfish desires and ambitions that once enslaved you.

# Conclusion

**1 Peter 4:7-8** *But the end of all things is at hand; therefore be serious and watchful in your prayers. And above all things have fervent love for one another, for "love will cover a multitude of sins."*

You close this principle by examining two verses from the First Epistle of Peter. He gives you a solemn admonishment by stating the end of all things is near. This simply means what it states, that is, the end is nearer than you might think.

You are told in the letter to the Romans the end is nearer than first believed. **Romans 13:11**, *"And do this, knowing the time, that now it is high time to awake out of sleep; for now our salvation is nearer than when we first believed."* Both Paul and Peter are trying to show you the need to apply the principles of Christianity and the Bible to your life in daily practical living, not the philosophies the world or the twelve steps of anonymous groups teach about being sober. The lifestyle of Christianity and the Bible addresses all of life's issues and gives clear and simple instructions for living a sober way of life.

Peter is trying to communicate your need to daily seek after God for a life of sobriety. You are to be watchful in your prayers, you are to lean upon God for all things and allow Him to guide and instruct you. **Proverbs 3:5-6**, *"Trust in the Lord with all your heart, and lean not on your own understanding; in all your ways acknowledge Him, and He shall direct your paths."*

Peter says after you have received your instructions for daily living that you are to have fervent love for one another. This simply means the love you have is unceasing and supplied by God. It causes you to have a love that not only observes the needs of others, but also tries to meet those needs as best you can and what God will allow you to. The love will not only be merciful to the individual to whom you are trying to minister, but will also cause you to have a gentle and meek approach in presenting them a solution to their afflictions, trials, and tribulations. You will be even much more sympathetic and empathetic to their suffering. You will love much and be merciful to others because you have received both from a living, loving, and merciful God.

## Questions for Lesson 8

1. What four items manifest within your life verify you have changed? Where does this change take place?

2. Describe the supernatural circulatory system and how it works.

3. What is the natural result of being found in Christ? How does this result take place? Is it accomplished by your own will power or design? How long does it take to overcome this plight?

4. What are the results of practicing the Lord's principles in your life?

5. In your own words, describe the difference between worldly pity and heavenly pity? How has your understanding of these two definitions changed you and your outlook on your need of God's pity now?

6. What is the definition of comfort?

7. What is the definition of tribulation?

8. What is the definition of restore? What does it mean in an ethical sense?

9. What is the definition of meekness?

10. What is the definition of consider?




11. What are the positive and negative definitions of tempted?




12. What is the number one temptation you face when you try to help others who are just entering into the practice of living in sobriety?




13. What are the two weaknesses that face and confront you?




14. What is at the heart of your desire to serve others?




15. What is the meaning of being watchful in your prayers?




16. In your own words, describe what serving others means to you now and what part it truly plays in your sobriety. Why is it an important part of being sober?

# Drawn by Christ

I was born and raised in Mississippi and have lived throughout the United States, though mostly in the Northwest. I now call Boise my home and am answering God's call in my life to minister to those who are dealing with addictions of any type and currently to men incarcerated in the county jail.

The son of devout Southern Baptists, I attended church three times a week throughout my childhood. As a teenager, I completely rebelled against my parents' way of life and threw myself headlong into a lifestyle characterized by heavy drinking and drugging along with a variety of criminal activities to support my growing drug habit. After several brushes with the law, I joined the Army at 19 in an attempt to turn my life around. Upon being discharged from the Army, I moved to Idaho where I obtained a degree in Business and Accounting from BSU. Shortly before I graduated, I married my girlfriend of four years. By all outward appearances, I was leading a successful life but on the inside and to those who really knew me, my life was a living hell of alcohol and drug addiction. I simply could not quit drinking and drugging, no matter how hard I tried or how badly I wanted to. My wife and I would have knockdown, drag-out fights after nights of drinking myself into a stupor. After two years of marriage, my wife left me and eventually, we divorced.

This was the straw that broke the camel's back and tore down my walls of denial. Shortly after she left me, I got down on my knees and begged God to forgive me for turning my back on Him. I was delivered from drugs and alcohol that evening and have never looked back (almost 19 years ago). I spent two years attending AA meetings, but knew inside that AA would not be able to help me build and grow my relationship with Jesus Christ. In 1989, I attended my first Pure Word meeting at Calvary Chapel with my future bride. I knew instantly Christ had drawn me to this program and that, at last, I was home.

I have been with the same employer for almost 19 years working as an accountant and financial analyst. I have been actively involved with various prison/jail ministries for 11 years, and have been serving as an elder of Pure Word Ministries for several years. My greatest desire is to help others who are struggling with addictions to not only experience the freedom of overcoming their addictions but to also experience the joy and peace that can only come from a personal relationship with our Lord and Savior, Jesus Christ.

Bob

# Lesson 9: Relapse, The Problem and The Process (Part 1)

You have examined the twelve principles and their scriptural applications to your life. You observed the perspective of your problems from God's point of view by carefully examining them through the scriptures.

You learned what your present practice now should be as a new creation in Christ. You discovered God has provided a way out of your bondage from the ways of the flesh (sinful nature) by setting you free through grace and faith in Jesus. You then began to daily practice putting off the old man and all his ways. You learned the importance of dying to self and obeying the God-ordered priorities He has placed in man's life in order to give him the utmost in life. These are: Jesus first and others second. You learned if you practiced keeping these two items in their proper order, God would take care of all of your personal needs. The promises you received from God's Word and the new way of life He manifested within it have given you renewed hope. This helped you to pursue the necessary changes in your life despite the ongoing trials and tribulations that often occurred because of your putting off your old behaviors, allegiances, alliances, habits, and practices. It showed you the reality of your three enemies and their ongoing strategies to steal, destroy, and kill you. These enemies are: your flesh, this world and its philosophies and teachings, and finally, the devil.

The next important issue to look at is relapse or what the Bible calls "backsliding." You will study this for several reasons. The first is not to place you in fear of relapse happening to you but rather to show you it is not something to be <u>afraid of or unavoidable</u>. Relapse is an incident that can be avoided through the daily practice of Godly living, through regular Bible reading, prayer, accountability, fellowship, and serving first in the community of believers and secondly, serving the outside community.

You will see certain characteristics that transpire during this critical period. These are listed as a measuring tool and <u>not as something to suggest</u> you are now presently going through the process of relapse. Some of these items occur during normal everyday life in the form of temptations. Other characteristics, when put together in a chain of events, can be the cause of avoidable, but common, occurrences during the learning period of putting into practice regular Godly living habits. Remember, you have had a long period of time to practice what has brought you into bondage. It may have been a lifetime of practice or perhaps just a short time – it doesn't really matter. The flesh doesn't need a lot of time to make a habit of something. Remember what **Romans 6:16** states, "*Do you not know that to whom you present yourselves slaves to obey, you are that one's slaves whom you obey, whether of sin leading to death, or of obedience leading to righteousness?*"

You will also learn about reasoning processes and ungodly habits that may contribute to a backslidden condition. Thinking errors or the foundation of your beliefs is not the only thing that needs to be addressed in order to bring about permanent change or that just a behavioral change is required to give a balanced and fruitful life of sobriety. It takes a change brought about only through receiving the precious gift of sobriety from God who gives perfect and unchanging gifts that bring life not only to the individual, but also to those who surround him.

In closing this introduction, you should pray and ask the God of life to prepare your heart and clear your conscience so you will learn from these lessons. Please remember He has called you to freedom and has made way for you to be free from fear and worry. He has given you power, a sound mind, a sincere faith, and a clean conscience. He has promised you a good and fulfilling life if you'll remain abiding in Him. He knows your needs and your future, and He has promised a future that will be good for you.

Lastly, please remember relapse doesn't have to be a part of your life or in your future. It might be you may be called on to minister to someone who has fallen into this trap. If this is the case, then you will need to learn why and how it happened. In doing so, you may learn how to prevent it from happening in your own personal life.

## Relapse/Backsliding

The Christian walk is full of blessings, trials, and tribulations. It requires the Christian to take an inventory of himself on a daily basis. The Apostle Paul instructed you to judge yourself so you would not be judged. David petitioned the LORD in the Psalms to search him, know him, and lead him in the way of righteousness.

There are times in a Christian's life when the cares of this world, the deceitfulness of riches, the desire for other things, and even the cares for your family turn your focus away from your first love. These seasons would harden your heart to the things of faith and the work of belief if it were not for the grace and mercy of God working sovereignly in your life. When these seasons begin to take root in a Christian's life, the Bible addresses this as <u>backsliding</u>. In the life of a recovering drug addict or alcoholic, this series of events is called <u>relapse</u>. Relapse is <u>not</u> short periods of being dry followed by using again. (Drugs are defined in this study as alcohol, pharmaceuticals used in an illicit fashion, or anything mind-altering, whether it is manufactured or natural.)

**Relapse:**    In order for a relapse to occur you must <u>leave</u> the foundation of sobriety, the condition or state of mind of wellness that has provided testimonies from others and the assurance from God that your life has changed. This foundation includes effective personality and behavioral changes that are practiced daily.

This study will help you to clearly identify the causes, characteristics, and consequences of relapse. It will also help you to avoid the attitudes, circumstances, and mind games that plague the backslider. The last section will discuss the solution to the problem of relapse and give steps to help keep you on the path of righteousness for your own sake and for the sake of those you love.

Before you can understand the problem of relapse, you need to understand the nature of man. The concept of the "temple structure" of man uses a diagram with a series of concentric circles to illustrate the nature of man. The innermost circle represents the <u>spirit</u> or the <u>core of man</u>. The second area or circle houses the <u>soul</u>. The soul is made up of three sub-areas known as the <u>mind</u>, the <u>will</u>, and the <u>emotions</u>. The outermost circle represents the <u>body</u>. The <u>heart</u> refers to the whole of a person's being—both the spirit and the soul. See ***The Psychological Makeup of Man,*** Appendix 1, and ***The Structure of Man,*** Appendix 2.

**Proverbs 4:23** *Keep your heart with all diligence, for out of it springs the issues of life.*

**Romans 10:10** *For with the heart one believes unto righteousness, and with the mouth confession is made unto salvation.*

The Bible declares all decisions are settled in the heart. However, the cognitive or thinking process is completed in your brain; scripturally, this is known as your soul. The books of Proverbs and Romans declare you should guard your heart with all diligence because that is where the decisions of life and salvation are made.

**Matthew 15:18-19** *But those things which proceed out of the mouth come from the heart, and they defile a man. For out of the heart proceed evil thoughts, murders, adulteries, fornications, thefts, false witness, blasphemies.*

**Jeremiah 17:9** *The heart is deceitful above all things, and desperately wicked; who can know it?*

The matter of sin begins <u>with</u> and <u>in</u> your heart. Though the attitude of relapse manifests itself in many ways, it always begins in the heart and spreads to your thoughts, words, and actions.

**Psalms 51:5** *Behold, I was brought forth in iniquity, and in sin my mother conceived me.*

**Psalms 58:3** *The wicked are estranged from the womb; they go astray as soon as they are born, speaking lies.*

You are by nature a sinner. You didn't have to be taught or trained to sin; sin is habitual for you. You are trained to react and respond with the world's reactions. As a sinner, it was molded at birth; you are patterned after the first sinners—Adam and Eve (Ephesians 2:1-3).

In the book of Job, God asks the all-important question. **Job 14:4**, "*Who can bring a clean thing out of an unclean? No one!*" Your mind and heart have been skewed or scarred in their thinking and decision-making patterns since the fall of mankind. You are powerless in and of yourself to change that. Since Adam, the prototype of man, was scarred when he fell into sin, all men patterned after him have been scarred ever since. **Genesis 5:1-3**, "*This is the book of the genealogy of Adam. In the day that God created man, He made him in the likeness of God. He created them male and female, and blessed them and called them Mankind in the day they were created. And Adam lived one hundred and thirty years, and begot a son in his own likeness, after his image, and named him Seth.*"

**Romans 5:12** *Therefore, just as through one man sin entered the world, and death through sin, and thus death spread to all men, because all sinned...*

You are accustomed to, trained in, and practiced at being a sinner. You sin because that is who and what you are. Your sinful actions do not always result because you have learned or planned in your mind to sin (Romans 7:20). Your problems have not only been caused by a faulty foundational set of beliefs or your underprivileged environment. Jesus said in **John 8:34**, *"Most assuredly, I say to you, whoever commits sin is a slave of sin."*

Relapse does not begin with the action of again using drugs or alcohol after you have been drug or alcohol-free for a season. It begins in the heart and then affects the mind—in the way you think and make decisions. Your heart and mind have been flawed from the beginning, and you are powerless to change them. **Jeremiah 13:23**, *"Can the Ethiopian change his skin or the leopard its spots? Then may you also do good who are accustomed to do evil."*

**Jeremiah 22:21** *I spoke to you in your prosperity, but you said, 'I will not hear.' This has been your manner from your youth, that you did not obey My voice.*

God states the cause for this attitude and problem. According to this verse, when did the problem begin? When does it usually begin within you? When you are young at heart, right? So once again the Bible proves to be true when it declares *"Foolishness is bound up in the heart of a child; the rod of correction will drive it far from him."*

You have only one hope and alternative. You must turn to God who can make all things new. You must be born from above. He must make you a new creature. He alone can perform the supernatural change in your nature and character. This is the work of the Holy Spirit and it results in regeneration (Ezekiel 36:26).

**John 3:5-8** *Jesus answered, "Most assuredly, I say to you, unless one is born of water and the Spirit, he cannot enter the kingdom of God. That which is born of the flesh is flesh, and that which is born of the Spirit is spirit. Do not marvel that I said to you, 'You must be born again.' The wind blows where it wishes, and you hear the sound of it, but cannot tell where it comes from and where it goes. So is everyone who is born of the Spirit."*

Regeneration is when the very life of God first enters the soul of man. Regeneration is the process performed by God that gives man a new heart and spirit. The Holy Spirit performs this work because of grace through faith when man believes in the work of God. Another term for this is <u>salvation</u> or being "<u>born again</u>." (John 1:13; Titus 3:5; John 6:29)

Once you are born again, you can and must remind yourself daily that you have become a new creation in Christ (2 Corinthians 5:17). You must learn to live as the new creation He has stated you are. You must learn to appropriate the gifts and resources He has sovereignly placed in your life. This is especially important during the first year of practicing sobriety, also known as holy living.

When you are born again, you are also sanctified. This is done through the power of the Holy Spirit and results from the truth that resides in God's Word. At salvation, you are sanctified completely but the proof of your sanctification is observed through your daily pursuit of God. Sanctification (to be set apart, and made holy and separate from sin, to grow in the grace of God) enables you to serve the Lord. Jesus completed the work of sanctification when He died for you on the cross. However, the process of sanctification is completed through your love of God, which is demonstrated by your daily obedience to Him through faith. Sanctification establishes your heart through the work of grace. It is a <u>daily</u> process in a Christian's walk. (1 Corinthians 1:30; 2 Timothy 2:21)

## The Problem

Relapse or backsliding is not a one-time event or set of circumstances. It occurs as a slow and deliberate process of deterioration. It erodes your foundation of sobriety and holy living. There are several causes of relapse/backsliding. These are your wrong priorities, your half-hearted efforts, and your double-mindedness.

**Revelation 2:1-4** *"To the angel of the church of Ephesus write, 'These things says He who holds the seven stars in His right hand, who walks in the midst of the seven golden lampstands: "I know your works, your labor, your patience, and that you cannot bear those who are evil. And you have tested those who say they are apostles and are not, and have found them liars; and you have persevered and have patience, and have labored for My name's sake and have not become weary. Nevertheless I have this against you, that you have left your first love."'"*

The first cause of relapse is confused priorities. God and those you love are no longer your first priority. You allow something else to get in the way of your focus on the Lord. The people of the church in Ephesus were doing all the right things except the most important one.

**Matthew 6:24** *No one can serve two masters; for either he will hate the one and love the other, or else he will be loyal to the one and despise the other. You cannot serve God and mammon.*

Another cause of relapse is a half-hearted effort in gaining sobriety. Jesus said you cannot serve two masters, and a half-hearted effort will use up your strength and resources. (2 Chronicles 25:2; Luke 9:62; Revelation 3:15-16)

**James 1:6-8** *But let him ask in faith, with no doubting, for he who doubts is like a wave of the sea driven and tossed by the wind. For let not that man suppose that he will receive anything from the Lord; he is a double-minded man, unstable in all his ways.*

The people in Hosea's time called on the Lord but their hearts were far from Him. They thought they were right before God and were truly worshiping Him but they were not worshiping Him in spirit and truth, they were double-minded. **Hosea 11:7**, *"My people are bent on backsliding from Me. Though they call to the Most High, none at all exalt Him."* Also read Isaiah 29:13.

If you don't actually do what the Word instructs you to do, you deceive yourself. **James 1:22**, *"But be doers of the word, and not hearers only, deceiving yourselves."*

Relapse most often occurs because you falsely believe your foundation of God's love has somehow been diminished or shattered. You relapse when your trust in God begins to erode. This causes you to turn to self and pursue your pleasures. When you confront the issue of relapse in your life, you must first understand the truth of God's love for you. <u>Reality</u> is not defined from <u>your</u> perspective. It is not how you think God sees you or what He thinks about you. <u>God's</u> knowledge and love for <u>you</u> define reality. He knows you completely—from beginning to end.

**Psalms 139:1-6, 13-18** *O LORD, You have searched me and known me. You know my sitting down and my rising up; You understand my thought afar off. You comprehend my path and my lying down, and are acquainted with all my ways. For there is not a word on my tongue, but behold, O LORD, You know it altogether. You have hedged me behind and before, and laid Your hand upon me. Such knowledge is too wonderful for me; it is high, I cannot attain it.... For You formed my inward parts; You covered me in my mother's womb. I will praise You, for I am fearfully and wonderfully made; marvelous are Your works, and that my soul knows very well. My frame was not hidden from You, when I was made in secret, and skillfully wrought in the lowest parts of the earth. Your eyes saw my substance, being yet unformed. And in Your book they all were written, the days fashioned for me, when as yet there were none of them. How precious also are Your thoughts to me, O God! How great is the sum of them! If I should count them, they would be more in number than the sand; when I awake, I am still with You.*

This accurate perspective of reality protects you from relapse. You must make God's Word and His love for you your number one priorities. You must believe His promises to fulfill His will in your life. If you have accepted and committed your life to Him as Savior and LORD, you must not take for granted His title of Savior and then forget He is also LORD. Remind yourself and others daily of this wonderful fact. Never forget what Jesus did and accomplished for you. (Ephesians 2:10; Phillipians 1:6; 1 Thessalonians 5:23-24; Hebrews 13:20-21)

Next, you'll see the characteristics that demonstrate the <u>deterioration</u> or <u>erosion</u> of a walk of sobriety. They happen as a process, not a one-time event. They all transpire in the battleground of your mind where this process affects your thoughts, words, and actions.

## Characteristics of Relapse

During the process of relapse, you begin to display certain characteristics. Characteristics are defined as your present day habits or practices. They are separate from your nature. They can be positive or negative because they are natural and are controlled by whatever controls the soul, either the Holy Spirit or the flesh. These include:

- denial of your symptoms or attitudes

- making excuses

- taking for granted your newly-found walk of peace and serenity

- a know-it-all mentality

- doubt

- fear

- anger

- depression

- unforgiveness

- resentment

- rebellion

- stubbornness

- bending of the rules

- a judgmental attitude

- self-pity

- procrastination

- an "I don't care" attitude

- an "it won't happen to me" attitude

- defeatism

- laziness/apathy

- a "victim" mentality

- sabotage

## Sabotage

Let's look more closely at the last characteristic: sabotage. Sabotage is the deliberate damaging of progress of one's personal achievements. The person in relapse who exhibits this characteristic actually sabotages his own life. He destroys or hampers his own progress because of a <u>fear of responsibility</u>.

An example of this is someone who is walking in sobriety and begins to do very well at his job. He is offered a promotion. Instead of taking the promotion and trying his best, he becomes afraid of success and decides not to show up to work for a few days. Instead of being promoted, he gets fired. He sets himself up for failure.

Sabotage can frequently occur in the early stages of recovery. If allowed to be practiced, it can become a habit and can permanently scar one's character and history for the future. It can occur anytime during your new life in Christ, but most frequently, sabotage occurs during the first two or three years. It can cause the erosion or collapse of your sobriety. The root cause may be laziness and refusing to practice holiness in your thoughts, words, and actions on a daily basis. It can also be caused by fear and a buildup of unresolved resentments, resulting in bitterness.

In the process of sabotage, a person's focus turns away from the things of God to the things of the earth, and the enemy overwhelms him with self-condemnation. He is frustrated with his inability to measure up to his and other's expectations and his inability to follow through with these expectations. He expresses his own inner turmoil through sarcasm and criticism of others.

He measures himself falsely in three ways. First, he puts too much emphasis on his failures. Secondly, he puts too much confidence in his successes, and, thirdly, he miscalculates the rate and progression of his backsliding.

Sabotage results in isolation. Because of pride, the individual stops talking about the matters affecting him and is deluded about his foundation of sobriety. He is tempted to leave the environment that has developed around him and will attempt to go back to what was comfortable, such as old habits, alliances, and hangouts. The heart of the individual is tempted to shift the blame to others and to justify, minimize, and rationalize his behavior. If he remains on this course, his heart will grow cold and unresponsive to the conviction of the Holy Spirit.

The solution to this crisis is to stay accountable on a daily basis to people who love you. You need to discover the triggers that cause the temptation to run. This habit is usually traceable to unsuccessful attempts at sobriety in the past. And, of course, you need to be obedient to the Word of God. One of the liberating results of obeying the Word of God is the ability to look at and learn from the events that have transpired in your past <u>without</u> condemnation.

When you are humble in heart—the result of this new character developing within you—you are now able to not take yourself so seriously. Although you take your mistakes seriously, you are now able to look at them in the light of God's grace and mercy. You know His love covers a multitude of sins. You are able to think clearly about your mistakes and to discern why you made them—without fear and anxiety. You can now refuse the temptation to run and, instead, think through and discuss your options with your discipler. You begin to desire to learn a new way of living with an eagerness to be responsible and accountable.

God's Word has much to say about the whole process of relapse or backsliding. Read Joshua 23:11-16 to see the behaviors and patterns of backsliding. Look for the characteristics and see if you can identify them.

**Ezekiel 18:26** *When a righteous man turns away from his righteousness, commits iniquity, and dies in it, it is because of the iniquity which he has done that he dies.*

If you don't forsake your old alliances, old friendships, and old behaviors, God will not override your will or choices. These alliances will grow like weeds and soon take over all the good seed you have planted. God reminds the children of Israel He is trustworthy, truthful, and faithful. He will be faithful to bless them but He is also faithful to allow the negative consequences of their choices.

At the core of the process of relapse sits <u>pride</u>. Pride causes you to persuade yourself, and sometimes others, to depend upon and to use all sorts of excuses. The excuses try to justify, rationalize, and minimize your sinful behavior. In reality, they only serve to magnify your sinful attitudes. Ultimately, pride causes you to turn away from God and to accept the philosophies of the world.

Your fleshly nature longs to turn to self and trust in your own heart (Jeremiah 17:9). Your own thoughts and motives begin to drown out the voice of the Lord so you can no longer hear Him through your conscience. You fail to learn from your past mistakes, and you begin to forget the examples of others whom God has mercifully placed in your life. Relapse eventually kills. (Jeremiah 16:12)

Pride also affects your knowledge. **Isaiah 48:6-7** illustrates what happens, *"You have heard; see all this. And will you not declare it? I have made you hear new things from this time, even hidden things, and you did not know them. They are created now and not from the beginning; and before this day you have not heard them, lest you should say, 'Of course I knew them.'"*

Notice what your loving God states in the phrase: *"Lest you should say, 'Of course I knew them.'"* He knows what lies in the heart of man. He knows you sometimes get "all knowed up," that is, you think you know it all! Look at the warning from the scriptures concerning this attitude. **1 Corinthians 8:1b**, *"Knowledge puffs up, but love edifies."* (1 Corinthians 8:2)

**Proverbs 14:14** *The backslider in heart will be filled with his own ways, but a good man will be satisfied from above.*

You become obsessed with your own ways and begin to lose trust in everyone. Your sin increases, and the weight of sin holds you down and keeps you from making strides forward. (Isaiah 1:4; Hebrews 10:38)

Relapse/backsliding also causes you to isolate yourself. **Proverbs 18:1-2**, *"A man who isolates himself seeks his own desire; he rages against all wise judgment. A fool has no delight in understanding, but in expressing his own heart."*

**Jeremiah 6:28** *They are all stubborn rebels, walking as slanderers. They are bronze and iron, they are all corrupters;...*

Your pride results in stubbornness and slander. God identifies the character of these people, he calls them rebels. Their problem is not being rebellious as in earlier passages. These people had become so <u>practiced</u> at rebelling that their character had been trained to rebel—it had became their habit. The problem He addresses here is their stubbornness.

Pride causes you to walk about in presumption. You slander those around you because you falsely assess their character. This is usually brought about because of your own envy, covetousness, or insecurity. You end up judging the hearts of others when you need to be allowing God to search your own heart.

**Jeremiah 7:26** *Yet they did not obey Me or incline their ear, but stiffened their neck. They did worse than their fathers.*

Relapse causes a loss of ability to hear and obey. When you fall back to the ways of the flesh, you end up worse off than when you started. Before Christ's atonement for your sin, there was no relief for the things you had done, and the curse of your sin continued through the generations.

**2 Peter 2:20-21** *For if, after they have escaped the pollutions of the world through the knowledge of the Lord and Savior Jesus Christ, they are again entangled in them and overcome, the latter end is worse with them than the beginning. For it would have been better for them not to have known the way of righteousness, than having known it, to turn from the holy commandment delivered to them.*

You begin to listen to whatever makes you feel good, whether that be ungodly counsel, the world's philosophy, or your own heart. You turn to a <u>sensory</u> or <u>sensual</u> type of faith rather than a foundational, scriptural-based faith. You turn back to old alliances, old patterns, and the rut from which you were delivered. You lie to yourself and to others to cover your sin, and your rut soon turns to a grave. All of your resources are used up, depleted, or carried away. **Hosea 12:1**, *"Ephraim feeds on the wind, and* *pursues the east wind; he daily increases lies and desolation. Also they make a covenant with the Assyrians, and oil is carried to Egypt."*

**1 Corinthians 15:33** *Do not be deceived: "Evil company corrupts good habits."*

Unhealthy relationships can cause relapse but can also be a characteristic of this process. Relationships and associations with evil people can be extremely deceiving and destructive. The opposite is also true— **Proverbs 13:20**, *"He who walks with wise men will be wise, but the companion of fools will be destroyed."*

You can tell the difference between a wise friend and an evil acquaintance by their fruits. **Matthew 7:16-20**, *"You will know them by their fruits. Do men gather grapes from thorn bushes or figs from thistles? Even so, every good tree bears good fruit, but a bad tree bears bad fruit. A good tree cannot bear bad fruit, nor can a bad tree bear good fruit. Every tree that does not bear good fruit is cut down and thrown into the fire. Therefore by their fruits you will know them."*

**1 Kings 11:1-4** *But King Solomon loved many foreign women, as well as the daughter of Pharaoh: women of the Moabites, Ammonites, Edomites, Sidonians, and Hittites—from the nations of whom the LORD had said to the children of Israel, "You shall not intermarry with them, nor they with you. Surely they will turn away your hearts after their gods." Solomon clung to these in love. And he had seven hundred wives, princesses, and three hundred concubines; and his wives turned away his heart. For it was so, when Solomon was old, that his wives turned his heart after other gods; and his heart was not loyal to the LORD his God, as was the heart of his father David.*

Do not think you are above being corrupted by unhealthy relationships. Look what happened to King Solomon, one of the wisest men who ever lived. Relationships can alter your focus. If not put into proper perspective, they can cause rapid destruction in your life. If you are not rooted and grounded in Christ, your sobriety can be quickly undone. The result can often have a ripple effect on the generations to come.

Your emotions represent one of the most vulnerable areas in building a foundation of sobriety. They have been sheltered and inhibited from the moment you began using in a habitual manner. While you work on building a foundation of sobriety, your emotions beg to be set free and to experience life at its fullest. However, since they've been inhibited for so long, your emotions are immature. Your emotional age is, in fact, whatever age you were when you first began to use. Therefore, your emotions need strict governing, guidance, and accountability. (See *The Anniversary Periods,* Appendix 5.)

The devil cannot capture the spirit of a man once the Holy Spirit indwells him so he tries to influence the next best thing—the emotions. The most effective tool the devil uses to attack your emotions is through your sexuality. Once you have been born again, your body becomes the temple or tabernacle of God. Satan uses your sexuality to tempt you into sexual sin, which causes you to blaspheme the temple of God. Sexual sin is the only sin you commit against your body. The enemy of your soul would like nothing better than for you to damage your body in one lethal form or another, and sexual sin is one of the best ways for him to get this done. (See *The Psychological Makeup of Man*, Appendix 1.) (1 Corinthians 6:18-19)

**Romans 7:15, 19** *For what I am doing, I do not understand. For what I will to do, that I do not practice, but what I hate, that I do. For the good that I will to do, I do not do; but the evil I will not to do, that I practice.*

The area of sexuality is the most personal, guarded, or secretive area in your life. It is also the most vulnerable. As you learned in earlier lessons, when you are told not to do something, the rule of law is birthed within you, and you automatically desire to do what you are told not to do.

The area of sexuality is one of the most coveted areas the devil desires to control. Again, remember you are the tabernacle in which the Holy Spirit dwells (1 Corinthians 6:18-19). Because of this, it serves Satan well when he brings blaspheming and railing accusations when he accuses you before your Father in heaven on account of your sinful behaviors, words, and deeds. He also incites within you the desire to rebel against the ownership of God who purchased your spirit, soul, and body through the sacrifice of Jesus on the cross.

Secondly, Satan uses your sexuality as a tool against you because of its location (just outside your core, see Appendix 1). Satan knows your need to relate and be needed. Through this area, he can gain an almost unbreakable control of your <u>will</u> and nature. Satan can build a wall of separation between you and God's sovereign purpose to save you because of the strong grip <u>pleasure</u> plays in your being.

The secondary response that plays a powerful part in all of this is the area of <u>emotions</u>. Pleasure causes the drive behind the sinful behavior, and the emotions cause the reasoning behind the justification of the sinful behavior. These two powerful sophistries seem to originate from your heart, which at the time appear tried and true. During trials and tribulations of relapse, they try to take control. By combining both (emotions and pleasure), the devil has a potent combination to bring forth condemnation, guilt, and shame. He then uses these as barriers to keep you from believing in a loving, merciful, and forgiving God. God will wash away all of your sins at a moment's notice, if you will just repent, turn, and ask Him to forgive you.

Because you possibly have been flippant and reckless in this area of your life in the past and driven by your various lusts, you unintentionally and often ignorantly harmed your soul during the various acts of fornication. The harm done could be illustrated like this: picture gluing two different pieces of colored paper together – one, your favorite color (to represent you) and the other, a different color (to represent someone in your life). As you picture the gluing process in your mind, let it set, and then take the colored side representing you and grab a corner. Then have someone grab the corner opposite you. Now, gently take a corner and try to tear the two pieces of paper apart without doing damage to either side. Is it possible? Of course not!

The damage is obvious and, at times, significant. This is what happens to the souls of individuals when two people have sexual intercourse outside of marriage. They have nothing to hold them or bind them together, and, therefore, when they separate, they end up tearing their souls. This is repeated every time the act of fornication occurs.

It also causes more and more damage to occur with repeated actions of this nature. For illustration's sake, it also causes more "colors" to be added to your soul each time the act occurs. Thus, when it comes to imprinting upon your mate at the time of marriage, there are various colors and unwanted levels of memories and experiences that have to be forgotten (which is an impossibility). With a cluttered memory (possibly from a painful and damaged past), experiences in guilt, shame, and often, condemnation, these issues and concerns can get in the way of a pure relationship with your future spouse. They can be an enormous hurdle to overcome as you try to gain an equal footing in your new relationship. By now, I hope you can see the obvious reasons for not having sexual intercourse before marriage. Here's another reason.

The brain is the most powerful organ in the world and has a design copyrighted by God Himself. Its ability to remember is remarkable. It has the power to move you through time and space back to the very moment when you first experienced a significant moment. The only problem with this tremendous ability is it can occur during the wrong time and place. You will desire your spouse to have a clear and clean response to you with memories only you two will share. However, in dealing with the past, the struggle to keep your mind on the present will be a constant trial. It will be an added burden to the marriage relationship and one that will, more than likely, be dealt with through isolated, mental suffering for fear of being rejected by the spouse because of such thoughts and temptations. It will take a longer season of time to make a new bank of memories to replace the memories of the past and an additional time of suffering in order to accomplish this.

The ideal for marriage is to have a smooth surface on your soul, one that offers no blemish, contamination, or soiled surface. Remember the covenant of marriage is binding for a lifetime. Because there is no immediate pain or tragic consequence, individuals have a tendency to think they have escaped the consequences of their actions of the moral foundation they have learned (e.g., Sunday school, education, parental warnings). But in reality, just like the fall of mankind in the garden, Adam and Eve died immediately (spiritually) and didn't know it, so it also is with sexual intercourse outside of marriage. You end up harming your most vulnerable commodity – your soul. Because you don't feel or see the harm right away (remember, sexually transmitted diseases [STDs] are not always detected immediately), you end up thinking you have somehow escaped the surveillance of God's watchful eye. Remember, God has set forth in His creation laws and principles that govern both mankind and creation. One of these is the spiritual principle of sowing and reaping. **Galatians 6:7-8**, *"Do not be deceived, God is not mocked; for whatever a man sows, that he will also reap. For he who sows to his flesh will of the flesh reap corruption, but he who sows to the Spirit will of the Spirit reap everlasting life."*

The reason the Word of God states sexual intercourse is supposed to be saved only for the marriage relationship is because of its importance to the well being of the institution of the family and society. When this most holy and sanctified act takes place between the husband and wife, they are to be, idealistically, virgins so they can imprint upon each other. Imprinting means to be one, to leave a lasting image and impression, to implant firmly on the mind. In the psychological arena, it means a learning mechanism operating very early in the life of an animal, in which a particular stimulus immediately establishes an irreversible behavior pattern with references to the same stimulus in the future. In other words, you are to have a clean slate to operate on in regards to learning about one another, especially in the area of sexuality between the spouses. If this is accomplished, your soul will have no damage to work through, and you will be pure. You will be able to cleave to one another with no distractions, memories, or experiences to foul your thought life. You will be one in purpose, vision, and hope.

# Conclusion

If relapse or sexuality immorality has been an area that has produced the results of doubt and unbelief to thrive within you, as well as a backlash of emotions, please remember what your loving God states about His love, mercy, and forgiveness. He has stated you are loved with a love, mercy, and kindness that are everlasting and unfailing. He tells you He thinks about you all the time, and His thoughts are precious and more numerous than all the stars. He has stated that through His compassion for you, you are not consumed, and if your own heart condemns you, He is greater than your heart and knows all things. He removes your sins as far as the east is from the west and in addition to this, He throws them behind His back, not yours. He allows you to start out every day with a fresh new batch of His compassion, love, and mercy. Lastly, He states the good work He has begun within you will be brought to completion. He will bring the glorious work of sanctification (which means to grow in His grace) to fulfillment by perfecting your spirit, soul, and body and making you blameless through His cleansing blood until the coming of your Lord and Savior. He is faithful, and He will do it.

So, as you learn to trust in your loving God and as you daily practice pouring out your heart to Him, you will learn through experiencing the fruit of His presence and the results of a productive, balanced, and abundant life. His Word is true and it is impossible for Him to lie. So praise Him and thank Him for His long-suffering, forbearance, and riches in goodness. Truly, your soul silently waits for God; from Him comes your salvation. He alone is your rock and your salvation; He is your defense; you shall not be greatly moved.

## Questions for Lesson 9

1. Why it is important for you to understand what relapse is?

2. What are the seven ingredients that will guarantee a full and abundant life in recovery? Which have taken place in your life? What difference have they made?

3. What four things can cause you to turn your attention and focus away from Christ? Have these ever affected you? How?

4. Where are all decisions settled or made: the mind or the heart?

5. When did your problems begin? Were you ever without sin? Will you ever be able to solve your issues with sin? Why or why not?

6. Does the issue of relapse begin with the action of using drugs or going back to your old behaviors?

7. What is the definition of sanctification?

8. Is relapse or backsliding a one-time event or set of circumstances and what are the causes?

9. What defines reality?

10. What is the definition of characteristics?

11. List some of your own specific characteristics of relapse.

12. In your own words, describe how sabotage has affected you and your walk in sobriety.

13. What is the solution to eliminating sabotage? Write down the plan you will use to help you establish a safety route through the valley of temptation? Be specific.

14. According to God's definition, what are some of the causes of backsliding or relapse?

15. What is at the core or heart of the issue of relapse?

16. Why do your feelings affect your faith and how do you avoid turning to or relying upon them? When you allow this reaction to occur, what are some of your actions or behaviors? What happens to your resources?

17. Why can relationships alter your focus? What is one of the most vulnerable areas and why is it vulnerable? What is the most effective tool the devil uses to attack your emotions?

18. What does your body become once you become "born again"? What is the only sin you commit against your body?

19. Why does the devil desire to gain control over your sexuality?

20. Where is the area of sexuality located? What three elements of your makeup does Satan desire to control? How do pleasure and emotions work in the process of justification?

21. What does imprinting mean and how does it operate within relationships?

# Foundation in the Lord

Looking back on my childhood is hard. It brings back a lot of pain as I had a very abusive father and a depressed, insecure mother who didn't protect us. My dad was a very angry man and everything set him off; he took most of it out on us kids. He would often pull out my hair or twist my lip until it bled for something as silly as spilling some water on the floor. He beat us with his belt almost daily. The sexual abuse was just as devastating. We belonged to a religious sect that knew about the physical abuse but encouraged my mom to work it out. By 15, I was drinking and having sex with my boyfriend. I was 17 the first time I smoked pot and a few months later was introduced to crank. I felt invincible, like I was finally in control. At first I only used on weekends, but after a few months I quit my job and became a full-time addict. I moved in with my aunt, who was also using meth.

I met David in 1996. We met during a deal and instantly hit it off. The next time we saw each other, I moved in with him and we got married. David was selling large quantities of crank. I realized my husband believed in God because he would read the Bible. I later found out he had given his life to Christ in high school, but had gone back to drugs a short time later.

Four months later, I got pregnant. I realized I wanted more for my life and for my baby, but David wasn't ready. Two months after our son was born, David had a warrant issued for his arrest. We ran, living in drug houses. When the police finally found us, they jumped out with their guns drawn. David told me, "It's done, I surrender." It wasn't until later I would fully understand what that meant. My husband says he wasn't "arrested," he was "rescued." God met David in the back of that police car, and David's heart was changed instantly.

Once David was in jail, he re-dedicated his life to Christ. God had completely taken all his cravings and he was fully delivered from his addiction. I wasn't buying his "jailhouse conversion." I didn't really know what to believe about God. It wasn't until I went to my husband's sentencing that I truly saw who God is and I saw Him work. As David stood before the judge, he told the judge he wanted to pay for his crimes. He said he deserved to go to prison and if sent there he would bring the gospel of Jesus to the men there. But he felt his first ministry was his wife and kids. I felt the presence of God in that courtroom and knew everything would be okay. I saw the judge's face soften and he sentenced David to 10 years with all of it, except 180 days, suspended. That meant David would be out in just a couple of months! I knew then God was watching over my husband.

David called that night and asked me to kneel on the floor and pray with him. I did, and I asked God to make me new, and He did! God completely delivered me from my drug addiction just as he did for David. Being involved in Pure Word has given us the foundation to grow our faith deeper and stronger in our Lord and Savior. It has brought us together in love for people who struggle with life-altering sin where we stand in the gap for those who need God's love and grace to be able to break the sin of addiction.

It has been almost seven years since I asked God to change my life and my heart and He has done just that! My husband and I have now been married for 8½ years and we have five children. It is our hearts' desire to reach as many hurting, addicted people as possible and bring them the good news of Jesus and His saving grace! How amazing it is to me that after all the horrible disgusting things I did, God washed it all away, and I am a new creation!

Amanda

# Lesson Ten: Relapse, The Process (Part 2) and the Solution

In this study on relapse, you have found it is not an occurrence that happens all at once. It is a slow and deliberate erosion of the foundation of established sobriety that has been developed and cultivated through the period of time that God, through grace and mercy, has provided you. You learned sobriety is a process that takes time and, often, periods of "longsuffering," also known as patience, in order to establish both quantity and quality. This change was a God-given gift from above and, as you are learning, it is orchestrated and controlled from above.

You looked at the important issue of having an accurate perspective of reality acquired through daily reading of God's Word and His unfailing love for you. You looked at the importance of allowing God to complete His wonderful work of sanctification (growing in His grace) to develop so your foundation of sobriety has time to mature.

You also looked at some of the traps you sometimes have a tendency to fall into, especially sabotage. You looked at the causes and the process of this destructive mind-set, and you saw the possible results of this action if allowed to fully develop in your life. The main factor that causes all relapse or backsliding was found to be <u>pride</u>. To quote the last lesson, *"Pride causes you to persuade yourself, and sometimes others, to depend upon and to use all sorts of excuses. The excuses try to justify, rationalize, and minimize your sinful behavior. In reality, they only serve to magnify your sinful attitudes. Ultimately, pride causes you to turn away from God and to accept the philosophies of the world."* Pride causes you to be presumptuous, dull of hearing, rebellious, stubborn, and insecure. It can cause you to turn to a sensory or sensual type of faith rather than a foundational, scriptural-based faith. If this occurs, it causes you to follow a pleasure-filled and emotionally based religion, rather than a faith based on God's Word and His Spirit.

In all of this, you must remember you are in the process of <u>learning</u> God desires to be intimately involved in every area of your life. He desires to lead you to victory through the knowledge of Christ as you escape and ultimately conquer the sinful nature, the world, and the devil. You are <u>learning</u> He allows trials and tribulations to afflict you in order to shape and mold, cultivate and strengthen, and lastly, to develop a sincere willingness and desire to have Him control you on a moment-by-moment basis. He holds your future, and He neither sleeps nor slumbers as He watches over you and cares for your every need. God's love is proven strong, faithful, and most importantly, everlasting as you endure and overcome all of life's daily circumstances and events.

In closing this introduction, please remember God's mercy is boundless and unlimited. Never be afraid to pour out your heart to Him, and never believe the temptation He is fed up with you or He won't forgive your sin. As you finish this section, please bear in mind you have a tendency at times to take yourself a little too seriously. Don't lose your sense of humor! Remember you are God's project, and you are a masterpiece in the works. **Ephesians 2:10**, *"For we are His workmanship, created in Christ Jesus for good works, which God prepared beforehand that we should walk in them."*

## The Process (Part 2)

**Luke 22:54-62** *Having arrested Him, they led Him and brought Him into the high priest's house. But Peter followed at a distance. Now when they had kindled a fire in the midst of the courtyard and sat down together, Peter sat among them. And a certain servant girl, seeing him as he sat by the fire, looked intently at him and said, "This man was also with Him." But he denied Him, saying, "Woman, I do not know Him." And after a little while another saw him and said, "You also are of them." But Peter said, "Man, I am not!" Then after about an hour had passed, another confidently affirmed, saying, "Surely this fellow also was with Him, for he is a Galilean." But Peter said, "Man, I do not know what you are saying!" Immediately, while he was still speaking, the rooster crowed. And the Lord turned and looked at Peter. And Peter remembered the word of the Lord, how He had said to him, "Before the rooster crows, you will deny Me three times." So Peter went out and wept bitterly.*

Peter shows you an example of the process of relapse in his denial of Christ. Look at his downward spiral. Identify the steps he goes through in the following accounts. (Matthew 26:69-75; Mark 14:66-72)

**Jeremiah 8:4-6** *"Moreover you shall say to them, 'Thus says the LORD: "Will they fall and not rise? Will one turn away and not return? Why has this people slidden back, Jerusalem, in a perpetual backsliding? They hold fast to deceit, they refuse to return. I listened and heard, but they do not speak aright. No man repented of his wickedness, saying, 'What have I done?' Everyone turned to his own course, as the horse rushes into the battle."'"*

The sin of relapse always has consequences. If you don't stop the process of relapse, <u>all areas of life begin to deteriorate</u> at an accelerated rate. The end condition of the individual becomes worse than the beginning. **2 Timothy 3:13**, *"But evil men and impostors will grow worse and worse, deceiving and being deceived."*

**Isaiah 1:22** *Your silver has become dross, your wine mixed with water.*

God desires purity from you but when you begin the process of relapse, you become skewed, convoluted, and confused. You lose your potency and become diluted. Have you ever seen inferior silver? Have you ever drunk watered-down alcohol? This illustrates what happens to your life when you become diluted in your sobriety.

When you <u>compromise</u> and do not do what is right in your Christian walk, you begin to lose your ability to influence by taste, light, and smell. Jesus warns you in the Sermon on the Mount. **Matthew 5:13-16**, *"You are the salt of the earth; but if the salt loses its flavor, how shall it be seasoned? It is then good for nothing but to be thrown out and trampled underfoot by men. You are the light of the world. A city that is set on a hill cannot be hidden. Nor do they light a lamp and put it under a basket, but on a* *lampstand, and it gives light to all who are in the house. Let your light so shine before men, that they may see your good works and glorify your Father in heaven."*

**2 Corinthians 2:15-16** *For we are to God the fragrance of Christ among those who are being saved and among those who are perishing. To the one we are the aroma of death leading to death, and to the other the aroma of life leading to life. And who is sufficient for these things?*

When you're walking in obedience to Christ, people can smell the fragrance of Christ in you. When walking in rebellion, what do you think they smell?

**Jeremiah 2:19** *"Your own wickedness will correct you, and your backslidings will rebuke you. Know therefore and see that it is an evil and bitter thing that you have forsaken the LORD your God, and the fear of Me is not in you," says the Lord GOD of hosts.*

Your own wickedness corrects you. This takes the blame game away. You are responsible for your own actions and cannot be the victim when it comes to your sin. You can't blame God or anyone else for getting busted. (Ezekiel 18:20; Numbers 32:23)

**Luke 12:2-3** *For there is nothing covered that will not be revealed, nor hidden that will not be known. Therefore whatever you have spoken in the dark will be heard in the light, and what you have spoken in the ear in inner rooms will be proclaimed on the housetops.*

When you are God's child, He lovingly cares for you and will do whatever it takes to ensure your salvation and your walk. When you try to do something in secret, God will expose and proclaim it in the light. (Luke 8:17; Psalms 32:3-4; Proverbs 28:13)

Why doesn't God let the little details go unseen or pass under His nose? Because He loves you and knows that <u>sin kills</u>! You don't always make the right choices, and, therefore, God sometimes has to discipline you because He loves you. If you try to cover up your sin, you will not prosper and your sin <u>will</u> find you out. Look at the following passage and identify the reasons why this is so important.

**Hebrews 12:6-11** *... for whom the LORD loves He chastens, and scourges every son whom He receives. If you endure chastening, God deals with you as with sons; for what son is there whom a father does not chasten? But if you are without chastening, of which all have become partakers, then you are illegitimate and not sons. Furthermore, we have had human fathers who corrected us, and we paid them respect. Shall we not much more readily be in subjection to the Father of spirits and live? For they indeed for a few days chastened us as seemed best to them, but He for our profit, that we may be partakers of His holiness. Now no chastening seems to be joyful for the present, but painful; nevertheless, afterward it yields the peaceable fruit of righteousness to those who have been trained by it.*

If you are His child, you will be disciplined. If you are not disciplined, you are an illegitimate child and not loved. Discipline shows you are loved, and you gain comfort and security from the boundaries discipline provides.

**Hosea 4:16-19** *For Israel is stubborn like a stubborn calf; now the LORD will let them forage like a lamb in open country. Ephraim is joined to idols, let him alone. Their drink is rebellion, they commit harlotry* *continually. Her rulers dearly love dishonor. The wind has wrapped her up in its wings, and they shall be ashamed because of their sacrifices.*

In this passage, the first issue is Israel's stubbornness. God compares His children to a stubborn calf. Because of their poor choices, God allows them to forage in open and unprotected lands. They are vulnerable prey for any predator. He allows Ephraim to keep his choices, his idols, and his drink. They commit spiritual adultery, and their authorities love dishonor more than honor. Again, they are told they will reap the wind because of their wickedness.


## The Solution

**Ezekiel 33:10-11** *"Therefore you, O son of man, say to the house of Israel: 'Thus you say, "If our transgressions and our sins lie upon us, and we pine away in them, how can we then live?"' Say to them: 'As I live,' says the Lord GOD, 'I have no pleasure in the death of the wicked, but that the wicked turn from his way and live. Turn, turn from your evil ways! For why should you die, O house of Israel?'"*

God is a very loving God and created you with free will—the ability to choose. He never takes away your choices and has promised He never will. He also lays before you the consequences of obedience versus disobedience: a blessing or a curse. You get to choose. (Deuteronomy 11:26-28; 30:15-20)

The key to victory over relapse is understanding the difference between <u>self-effort</u> versus being <u>filled with the Spirit</u> and then applying what you know.

You try to accomplish things in your own strength and find yourself lacking in strength, resources, and desire. You struggle in the flesh and resist in the spirit. In the carnal mind-set, you cannot operate with the mind of Christ. You are set upon your own resources, focus, and will, and you're settled upon what you are capable of accomplishing or can control. When you are in the flesh or depending upon yourself, you can count on three F's: fatigue, frustration, and failure.

On the other hand, when you are filled with the Spirit, you find yourself willing to put forth what seems to be supernatural effort to achieve or accomplish that which you set your mind upon. You are surrendered or resigned to the Lord's will and His leading. When you desire something and are filled with the Spirit, you surrender your will to the Lord to obtain it. You are more willing to ask for and accept prayer. You have an open mind-set and desire for accountability. You are teachable, humble, and broken in accepting whatever God desires to give you.

**Matthew 13:44-46** *Again, the kingdom of heaven is like treasure hidden in a field, which a man found and hid; and for joy over it he goes and sells all that he has and buys that field. Again, the kingdom of heaven is like a merchant seeking beautiful pearls, who, when he had found one pearl of great price, went and sold all that he had and bought it.*

Again, remember God's great love for you. You can do nothing to obtain salvation; you were bought at a price that only the Lord could pay.

**1 John 1:8-9** *If we say that we have no sin, we deceive ourselves, and the truth is not in us. If we confess our sins, He is faithful and just to forgive us our sins and to cleanse us from all unrighteousness.*

**Joel 2:13** *So rend your heart, and not your garments; return to the LORD your God, for He is gracious and merciful, slow to anger, and of great kindness; and He relents from doing harm.*

These passages illustrate and explain the need for the process of confession and repentance. Your heart is where healing must begin to take place. It does not start in your mind with your thinking. The heart is the birthplace of confession, repentance, and the origin of restoration. (Psalms 101:1-4; Hosea 6:1-2)

**Confession:** Admitting with your mouth and agreeing with God that you have done wrong.

**Repentance:** Turning away from sin and turning toward God.

**Restoration:** Being put back into right standing with God.

**Psalms 103:1-5** *Bless the LORD, O my soul; and all that is within me, bless His holy name! Bless the LORD, O my soul, and forget not all His benefits: who forgives all your iniquities, who heals all your diseases, who redeems your life from destruction, who crowns you with lovingkindness and tender mercies, who satisfies your mouth with good things, so that your youth is renewed like the eagle's.*

The result of genuine repentance is forgiveness, restoration, freedom, and healing.

**1 Peter 1:15-16** *…but as He who called you is holy, you also be holy in all your conduct, because it is written, "Be holy, for I am holy."*

God knows if your repentance is genuine. He desires you to be holy because He is holy. (Leviticus 11:44)

**Ezekiel 36:25-27** *Then I will sprinkle clean water on you, and you shall be clean; I will cleanse you from all your filthiness and from all your idols. I will give you a new heart and put a new spirit within you; I will take the heart of stone out of your flesh and give you a heart of flesh. I will put My Spirit within you and cause you to walk in My statutes, and you will keep My judgments and do them.*

This passage of hope shows how you become holy. You are not capable within your own power to complete this required task. God does this supernatural work for you and within you. God requires perfection, and you cannot achieve perfection on your own. (Ezekiel 11:19-20; Jeremiah 31:33-34)

**Romans 12:1-2** *I beseech you therefore, brethren, by the mercies of God, that you present your bodies a living sacrifice, holy, acceptable to God, which is your reasonable service. And do not be conformed to this world, but be transformed by the renewing of your mind, that you may prove what is that good and acceptable and perfect will of God.*

After God performs this work of restoration, you begin the process of renewing your mind. You accomplish this by daily washing your mind with the scriptures and the Holy Spirit. This is God's way of "brainwashing" you. (Hebrews 4:12; Titus 3:5-6)

The Word of God and the Holy Spirit perform the work within you. Only God, through the use of His Word, can accomplish this miraculous work. The Word has the power to divide the spirit from the soul so you can worship God in spirit and truth. It also allows you to understand what the Spirit says to you. Your mind needs to be washed and renewed through the Holy Spirit. God doesn't ask you to do anything unreasonable. He has already done everything for you and simply asks you to follow in His steps.

**1 John 2:15-16** *Do not love the world or the things in the world. If anyone loves the world, the love of the Father is not in him. For all that is in the world—the lust of the flesh, the lust of the eyes, and the pride of life—is not of the Father but is of the world.*

You must learn to resist the world and all of its influences. What does this mean? You should remain unblemished and undefiled from the world's philosophies or counsel. (Colossians 2:8, James 4:4)

You need God's help to offer things that are acceptable to Him. You need God's mercies in order to present yourself as a living sacrifice because you must be holy and acceptable to God. Only through the blood of Jesus can you be made clean and pure. Read Hebrews 9:19-28, especially verse 22. What astonishing truth about heaven! Christ's blood was even shed and spread over everything in heaven in order to provide and prepare safe and undefiled passage for you. Everything had to be purified, even in heaven, all your past, present, and future.

# Conclusion

As this study ends, be assured it has been a time that has stimulated you to learn from God's Word about His wonderful abilities to rebuild and restore all that seemed lost or destroyed. You now know and understand you can be restored. You have been given tools, not only for your own personal use, but also in the lives of others. You have a new vision and hope for the future.

By allowing God to perform His work of regeneration, sanctification, restoration, and renewal within you, you assure yourself of victory. No one can take the victory away from you, and no one else can take credit for it. For this, you give back to God all your praise, thanksgiving, and worship. You can now close with this blessing from **2 Thessalonians 2:16-17**, *"Now may our Lord Jesus Christ Himself, and our God and Father, who has loved us and given us everlasting consolation and good hope by grace, comfort your hearts and establish you in every good word and work."*

## Questions for Lessons 10

1. What two things give you an accurate perspective of reality?

2. What gives the foundation of sobriety the time to mature in your life?

3. What is the primary contributor that causes backsliding or relapse?

4. List the things Peter did to contribute to his denial of Christ. Matthew 26:69-75; Mark 14:66-72; Luke 22:54-62

5. What causes your descent into compromise?

6. What causes your correction – God or your own sin? Why can't you blame anyone else for your sin?

7. In the passage from Hosea 4:16-19 you see the results of being stubborn. What are the contributing factors listed as being the result of being stubborn?

8. What are some of the differences and results from when you operate in self-effort or the Holy Spirit? List them.

9. What does confession mean?

10. What does repentance mean?

11. What does restoration mean?

12. After the work of restoration is complete, what happens next?

13. How is the process of renewing your mind completed? What two things perform this work within you?

14. Why is it so important for you to resist the world and all its influences, philosophies, or counsel?

# Appendices
# And
# Answers to Lesson Questions

# Appendix 1

## The Psychological Makeup of Man

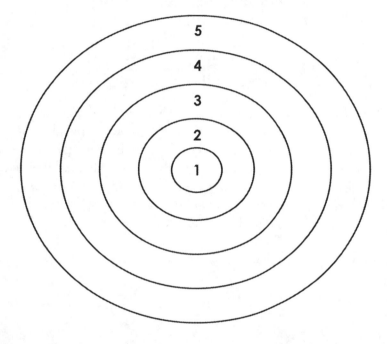

## Area 1 – Your Core

This area represents a God-shaped vacuum only God can fill or fit into. This area houses the spirit of man. The spirit within man remains dead until he becomes "born again." Only God can give life to the spirit of man. It is totally separate from the soul and body and when transformed, allows man to communicate with God. Only man has the ability and the desire to communicate with his Creator. Only man has a spirit that can be transformed and made alive. On the other hand, every living thing has a soul. Until God fills this core, you are preoccupied with self and left trying to fill it with the pursuit of anything else that would bring you pleasure. (John 4:24; Genesis 2:7; John 3:6; Ephesians 2:1; Colossians 2:13; John 6:53, 63)

**Zechariah 12:1** *This is the word of the LORD concerning Israel. The LORD, who stretches out the heavens, who lays the foundation of the earth, and who forms the spirit of man within him,…*

## Area 2 - Your Sexuality

This area is housed in your soul. Sexuality is the second most important area within man. It is what God gave to mankind to fulfill His relationship between man and woman. It is symbolic of the link Jesus has with the church and is to mirror the image of what a husband and wife are to share and project to the world in their marriage. You are called to nourish, guard, tenderly care for, keep pure, and dedicate your sexuality to one person only. Sexual immorality is the only sin you commit against the temple of God, which is your body. This area is so close to the center of your being or essence, that when awakened, if not governed by God, it soon enslaves your soul and rules your body. If not controlled, it will grow worse and worse in its downward path of lust. (Ephesians 4:22)

**1 Corinthians 6:18** *Flee sexual immorality. Every sin that a man does is outside the body, but he who commits sexual immorality sins against his own body.*

## Area 3 - Your Conscience and Will

This area is also housed in your soul. Your conscience and will allows you the ability to process interrelational issues within you. It is the place where your morals and values are developed. Before Christ, your morals and values are governed and exampled by your parents and authorities over you. You then make your judgments according to the foundation that has been built within you. At conversion, you surrender and submit these areas to the rule and reign of Jesus, who then begins the ongoing process of conforming and transforming them into His image. For a clear definition of what you are like before conversion in body and soul, read Romans, Chapters 1-3. (Hebrews 10:22)

**1 Timothy 1:5** *Now the purpose of the commandment is love from a pure heart, from a good conscience, and from sincere faith,...*

## Area 4 - Your Emotions

This area houses your creative and expressive abilities. The line between the two is indistinguishable. Your emotions allow you to develop and express your God-given personality traits. Remember, you were created in the image and likeness of God, and God has given you emotions to balance your nature and character. The nature and character areas are observed by the expression of your personality. Before conversion, this area (your emotions) is governed by the flesh and, at times, holds you in bondage. After conversion, it is governed either by the Spirit of God or by the flesh. Emotions were given as a way for mankind to reflect the image and goodness of God. The original purpose of emotions was to enhance the holiness and delight of our relationship with God. After the fall, they became clouded and began to reign and rule over the affairs of man. This resulted because of the fall and the corruption of the heart.

**Jeremiah 17:9** *The heart is deceitful above all things, and desperately wicked; Who can know it?*

Only the Word of God can bring separation between the spirit and soul of man. The soul houses the senses (emotions) of man and must be surrendered to the Holy Spirit. (Hebrews 4:12)

James states your carnal nature houses envy, self-centeredness, and bitterness, and unless controlled by the Spirit of God, you will be thrust into confusion and influenced by the world, the devil, and every ungodly thing. **James 3:14-16**, *"But if you have bitter envy and self-seeking in your hearts, do not boast and lie against the truth. This wisdom does not descend from above, but is earthly, sensual, demonic. For where envy and self-seeking exist, confusion and every evil thing are there."*

The word sensual could be translated feelings, emotions, or soul.

Another symptom and effect is listed in 1 Corinthians and gives you insight into the works of your carnal nature. Notice carnality hinders the growth and maturing process within you and causes the works of envy, strife, and divisions among you. **1 Corinthians 3:1-3**, *"And I, brethren, could not speak to you as to spiritual people but as to carnal, as to babes in Christ. I fed you with milk and not with solid food; for until now you were not able to receive it, and even now you are still not able; for you are still carnal. For where there are envy, strife, and divisions among you, are you not carnal and behaving like mere men?"*

## Area 5 – Your External Relationships

This area houses your ability to develop outside relationships with others. Until transformation and regeneration takes place through Christ, this area remains focused upon itself.

Narcissism is intrinsic to the flesh and cannot be overcome without the love of God to replace it. From the moment you are born again or transformed and renewed by the Spirit of God, you struggle with this issue and the Godly command to love others just as much as you already love yourself. (Mark 12:29-31; John 13:34-35; Ephesians 5:29)

**Luke 9:23-24** *Then He said to them all, "If anyone desires to come after Me, let him deny himself, and take up his cross daily, and follow Me. For whoever desires to save his life will lose it, but whoever loses his life for My sake will save it."*

# Appendix 2

## The Structure of Man

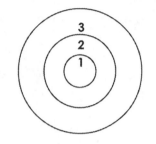

## 1= Spirit 2= Soul 3=Body

Man is divided into three separate and distinct divisions. This truth in illustrated in **1 Thessalonians 5:23**, *"Now may the God of peace Himself sanctify you completely; and may your whole spirit, soul, and body be preserved blameless at the coming of our Lord Jesus Christ."*

The three divisions are identified as spirit, soul, and body. They could be illustrated in many ways, but for the purpose of this example, they will be illustrated in the diagram above. To quote Watchman Nee, *"God dwells in the Spirit, self dwells in the Soul, and the senses dwell in the Body."* Although the lines that distinguish and divide them are virtually indistinguishable, all three exist because of what the scriptures state. The Spirit is where God dwells and is the source of life within man. (Genesis 2:7; 2 Corinthians 3:17)

**Zechariah 12:1** *The burden of the word of the LORD against Israel. Thus says the LORD, who stretches out the heavens, lays the foundation of the earth, and forms the spirit of man within him...*

## The Spirit: Conscience

Even though the spirit of man is dead in its natural fallen state of being, it houses within it the conscience, intuition, and communion.

The conscience is a sense of what is right or wrong in one's thoughts, actions, or motives. It is the discerning tool for right and wrong. The work of the conscience is independent and direct. Conscience is not to be confused with your ability to reason. Before regeneration, your reasoning often overrides your conscience and helps you to justify your sinful behavior. The evidence for the conscience is in the following scriptures: Romans 8:16; 1 Timothy 1:5; and Hebrews 10:22.

**1 Peter 3:21** *There is also an antitype which now saves us—baptism (not the removal of the filth of the flesh, but the answer of a good conscience toward God), through the resurrection of Jesus Christ,…*

## The Spirit: Intuition

The intuition is the perception organ in the human spirit. It is independent of any outside influence. It is knowledge that comes to you without any help from the mind, emotion, or volition (a.k.a. the will). It is a keen sense that manifests quickly. You know through your intuition; you understand through your mind. The evidence for the intuition is in the following scriptures: Matthew 26:41 and Mark 2:8.

**1 Corinthians 2:11** *For what man knows the things of a man except the spirit of the man which is in him? Even so no one knows the things of God except the Spirit of God.*

## The Spirit: Communion

Communion is the ability to and act of worshiping God. It is brought about by the transformation and regeneration of the repentant sinner. Communion directly corresponds with the regeneration of your spirit with the Holy Spirit. Holy Communion can only occur in the Spirit of the inner man and that only after being born again. It is independent and not associated with your carnal thoughts, emotions, or intentions. The will, intellect, emotions, or personality of unregenerate man cannot worship God on his own. It can, however, be active in unregenerate man as he worships evil principalities and powers that reside here on earth. It does not relate with the soul or carnal nature of man. The evidence for communion is in the following scriptures: Luke 1:47; John 4:23; and Romans 8:15.

**Romans 1:9** *For God is my witness, whom I serve with my spirit in the gospel of His Son, that without ceasing I make mention of you always in my prayers,…*

## The Soul

The soul is complex because housed within it is the mind, will, emotions, personality, and intellect. The soul will serve either the Spirit or the sinful nature because it always remains neutral. Whichever is ruling or reigning, the <u>Spirit</u> or the <u>sinful nature</u>, will control the soul. The soul houses <u>the will</u>. You are free to decide who or what you will serve. This explains your ability to have free will or choice. You were originally created to exercise your free will to love God but when the fall of man occurred, you exercised it and directed it toward yourself, rather than God. <u>Man was created morally innocent, not morally perfect</u>. The evidence for the free choice of man is in the following scriptures: Joshua 24:15 and Romans 6:11-12.

**Romans 6:16** *Do you not know that to whom you present yourselves slaves to obey, you are that one's slaves whom you obey, whether of sin leading to death, or of obedience leading to righteousness?*

The heart is often closely referred to in the same way as the soul and there is not always a clear differentiation between the two. You are told to guard it with all care. **Proverbs 4:23**, *"Keep your heart with all diligence, for out of it spring the issues of life."*

## The Body

The body is like the unregenerate heart; it can never be redeemed and will be done away with at the time of regeneration and reconciliation with God, face to face. God makes a new body in order to coexist with Him. (1 Corinthians 15:50, 53-55; 2 Corinthians 5:17; 1 Corinthians 1:29; 1 John 3:2)

**Ezekiel 36:26-27** *I will give you a new heart and put a new spirit within you; I will take the heart of stone out of your flesh and give you a heart of flesh. I will put My Spirit within you and cause you to walk in My statutes, and you will keep My judgments and do them.*

After being born again, you are commanded to honor God with your body because He purchased it.

**1 Corinthians 6:15-20** *Do you not know that your bodies are members of Christ? Shall I then take the members of Christ and make them members of a harlot? Certainly not! Or do you not know that he who is joined to a harlot is one body with her? For "the two," He says, "shall become one flesh." But he who is joined to the Lord is one spirit with Him. Flee sexual immorality. Every sin that a man does is outside the body, but he who commits sexual immorality sins against his own body. Or do you not know that your body is the temple of the Holy Spirit who is in you, whom you have from God, and you are not your own? For you were bought at a price; therefore glorify God in your body and in your spirit, which are God's.*

Everything will be created new. **Revelation 21:5**, *"Then He who sat on the throne said, "Behold, I make all things new." And He said to me, "Write, for these words are true and faithful."* (2 Peter 3:13; Revelation 21:1-2)

# Appendix 3

### Areas of Life

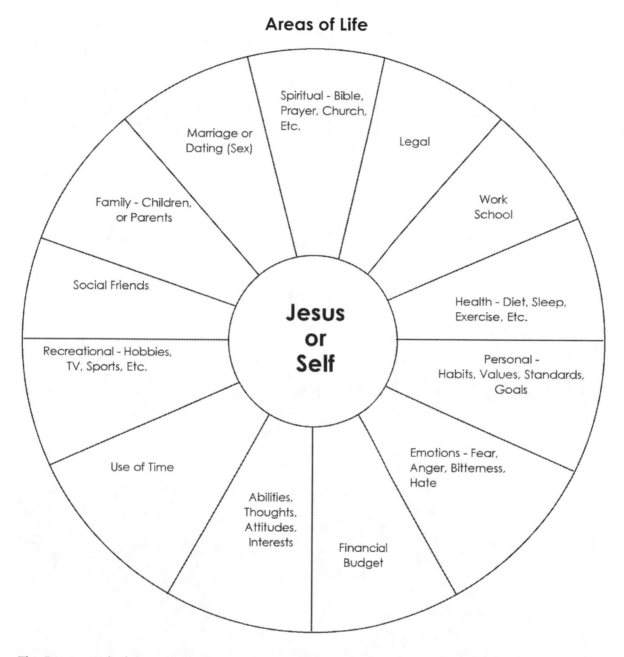

This Diagram only shows a small selection of the different areas of life we all have to balance and deal with. They can be governed by self or yielded to Jesus. Some will yield easily, others will be surrendered through tests, trials and tribulations. Only Jesus can balance all these areas at once. We can or will only focus on one or two areas at the most or at a time.

# Appendix 4

## Wheel of Emotion

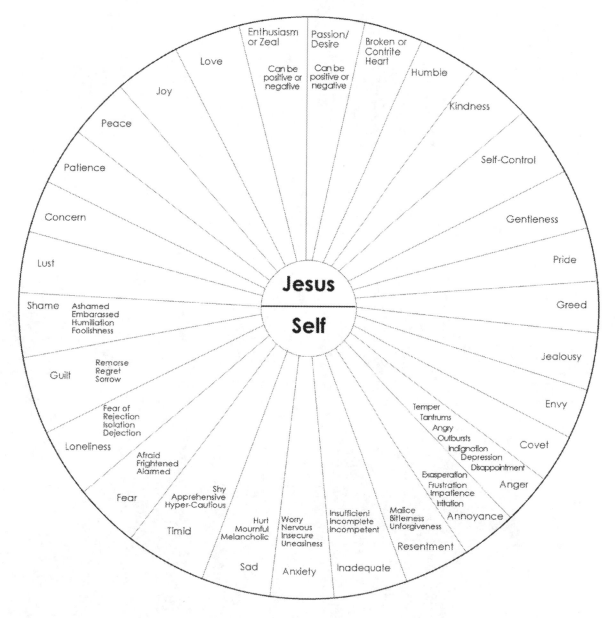

All these emotions can be used in either a positive or negative way. They can be either governed by self or yeilded to Jesus. They will produce one of two results: the works, acts or deeds of the sinful nature or the fruit of the Spirit.

# Appendix 5

## Anniversary Periods

The anniversary periods are notable times in early recovery you need to acknowledge and be sensitive to. It is during these times your emotions are the most powerful and, at times, cause an instability in rationale and emotions. They are as follows: 30 days, 60 days, 3 months, 6 months, 9 months, 12 months, 18 months, 24 months, 2.5 years, 3 years, 3.5 years, 4 years, 4.5 years, 5 years, 10 years, 15 years, etc. Five years is the accepted period of time in which a person is considered sober if he has maintained a continuous lifestyle of sobriety. After the fifth year it is statistically known, but not understood why, the anniversary periods fall in five-year intervals for the remainder of the life of the individual.

The physical body heals much sooner than the emotional area of your personality. See **The Wheel of Emotion**, Appendix 4. The emotional area of your being is arrested in its normal growth progression from the moment you begin to use in a habitual manner. Because of this, the first year is very emotional and tumultuous. You begin to experience more emotional upheaval in two areas, self-awareness and relationships. The first temptation you usually face is the emotion of loneliness and the desire for companionship. You are a relational creature and were created in the image and likeness of God. See **The Structure of Man**, Appendix 2. God is a relational being and you reflect that character.

When you discover who you are without the influence of a foreign substance corrupting your character or emotions, it is like a new drug to you and you often react to it that way. You want to explore these newfound feelings and share them with someone significant. You are zealous towards these newly aroused emotions and because you are without the trained and practiced strength to maintain and control them, you often fall prey to them quickly. You have always practiced the emotions of anger, bitterness, resentment, fear, and the like. If you have been acutely addicted, you usually have a tendency to become intensely aware of your sex drive, which was ignored because of your addictions. You have no balance, restraints, or boundaries in these areas. Because they are pleasure-based and occupy the second closest area to your core, the enemy desires to control them in any way he can. See **Psychological Makeup Of Man**, Appendix 1.

This is why most individuals are told or instructed to stay away from relationships within the first year. You barely know yourself emotionally without trying to get to know someone else on this level. This is like hooking up a horse to a buggy with the buggy in front. Relationships that are developed within the first year of recovery usually quickly gravitate to the physical or sexual arenas before the foundation of the relationship has a chance to fully mature. In addition to this, you are often totally unaware of the spiritual aspect of the law. When you are made aware of a behavior and told not to do it, you automatically desire to do it. This is known as temptation.

**James 1:14-15** *But each one is tempted when he is drawn away by his own desires and enticed. Then, when desire has conceived, it gives birth to sin; and sin, when it is full-grown, brings forth death.*

Sin affects three things that entice you to desire your own will or way. These are your will, imagination, and curiosity. Nothing from outside of you can affect your will except you. <u>No outside source can touch it.</u> You voluntarily have to open the doorway to it before it can be enticed.

You see how this works in the illustration of the fall of man in **Genesis 3:6**, *"So when the woman saw that the tree was good for food, that it was pleasant to the eyes, and a tree desirable to make one wise, she took of its fruit and ate. She also gave to her husband with her, and he ate."*

You'll notice Eve was enticed first to open her will, which she did by entertaining a conversation with the enemy. Second, she entertained her imagination by viewing the fruit and allowing it to entice her pleasures. Finally, her curiosity was enticed through the idea (a lie) she would be made as wise as God.

**Romans 7:14-23** *For we know that the law is spiritual, but I am carnal, sold under sin. For what I am doing, I do not understand. For what I will to do, that I do not practice; but what I hate, that I do. If, then, I do what I will not to do, I agree with the law that it is good. But now, it is no longer I who do it, but sin that dwells in me. For I know that in me (that is, in my flesh) nothing good dwells; for to will is present with me, but how to perform what is good I do not find. For the good that I will to do, I do not do; but the evil I will not to do, that I practice. Now if I do what I will not to do, it is no longer I who do it, but sin that dwells in me. I find then a law, that evil is present with me, the one who wills to do good. For I delight in the law of God according to the inward man. But I see another law in my members, warring against the law of my mind, and bringing me into captivity to the law of sin which is in my members.*

The first and foremost area the enemy wants to gain control over is the area of our will. The second is the area of our sexuality, the second area closest to the heart or center of man that only God can occupy. See ***Psychological Makeup of Man*** (Appendix 1). If Satan can gain control over this area, he can usually hinder growth in an individual for a considerable amount of time and, at times, cause irreparable damage or death.

You must first learn to die to self before you can get to know someone else. You need to be aware of who you are before you can truthfully be yourself with someone else.

There may be times when you react to something without knowing the cause for this reaction. You will then have to face the fear and anger caused by your insensitivity and unthinking behavior. You are self-centered and, just like an infant, you must learn self-control. You must grow and mature in your emotions and learn you have the ability to control them. You must begin to practice longsuffering before you are able to learn and experience what it does.

# Appendix 6

## The Dream Factor

**Job 33:14-18** *For God may speak in one way, or in another, yet man does not perceive it. In a dream, in a vision of the night, when deep sleep falls upon men, while slumbering on their beds, then He opens the ears of men, and seals their instruction. In order to turn man from his deed, and conceal pride from man, He keeps back his soul from the Pit, and his life from perishing by the sword.*

In early sobriety, dreams are one area you need to be aware of and may need to pay special attention to. Your newfound gift of sobriety, as well as your practice in sober living, will bring you joy beyond your imagination during the day. However, during sleep you may find an unexpected area of confrontation that can, if allowed, rattle your cage of understanding regarding your mental state. Dreams can sometimes cause a whole array of unknown and untouched emotions. If allowed to run unabated, they can truly unsettle you and cause you to go backwards for a time because of the fear and misunderstanding they cause.

You may never have been concerned about your dream life before. You have probably just had the undisciplined practice of letting your dreams continue without ever thinking, knowing, or understanding your ability to exercise self-control within them. More often than not they brought you pleasure; rarely did you ever have a bad dream. Now that you are beginning a new way of living and truly desire to live a life of sobriety in your thoughts, words, and actions, you'll sometimes find the devil has a new gated playground to try to gain access into. He will try to practice his wiles and schemes within your dreams to get you to accept his untruths. He will falsely accuse you and try to get you to believe in imaginary scenarios he has tempted you to believe are true.

## The Problem

Dreams can affect your psyche because they will tempt you into thinking you have someone or something to fear. Sometimes they will tempt you to think or feel you have used or even relapsed for a period of time.

Dreams come from a variety of sources: God, the devil, self, outside stimulants (food and drugs), and exhaustion. Dreams are a natural process within the accumulation of rest for the spirit, soul, and body. They can be imaginary or be made up of past events in your life. Dreams can be about incidents, specific time periods, individuals, and the tools you used in your dependency (e.g. relationships, needles, bongs, pipes, etc.). Dreams can also appear prophetic, sometimes referred to as déjà vu. Dreams will touch on what has brought you pleasure and what your heart may have loved the most. This experience can be confusing because of the pleasure factor in them. It is hard to give up something that has gone unrecognized as a danger and often it will lead you to want more time to sleep.

## The Time of Vulnerability

The usual time of vulnerability happens at about six months in the first year of practicing a life of sobriety. Dreams usually piggyback upon the feelings of victory over trials and tribulations that have appeared in the past as unconquerable. It is in these times of euphoria you are susceptible to falling in this area because you are not used to exercising or practicing self-control in your dreams. (1 Corinthians 10:12; Galatians 6:3.) It is in this area the devil often tries to dump condemnation on you because you feel bad for enjoying something you know beyond doubt has caused harm to your being and relationships. It is here you often encounter confusion and fear because you are tempted to think you have disappointed God or your loved ones because you found temporary pleasure in the moment and, at times, woke up in a hung-over state of mind.

## The Solution

When faced with this dilemma, you must do the following:

1)  Pray and prepare your mind for the time of sleep.
    a.  Read a passage of scripture and meditate on it rather than on something that transpired in your day, what you fear, fret, or are anxious about.
    b.  Avoid falling into bed and just going to sleep. Take time to give thanks to God for all He has given to you during the day.
    c.  Offer yourself up to God as a living sacrifice, even during sleep (Psalm 4:4-5; 63:6-7; 119:147-149; 143:5-6; Romans 12:1-2).
2)  Ask the Lord to fill you with His Spirit.
3)  Put on the whole armor of God with focus on the helmet of salvation. This protects your mind and follows the command that you are to protect the loins of your mind (1 Peter 1:13-14).
4)  Ask the LORD for wisdom in this area (James 1:5-6).
5)  Begin to practice self-control in this area (Galatians 5:23).
6)  Journal your victories for the days ahead, as well as for the testimony it will be for others.

Remember God is in control of all things, even your mind, and you must persevere in focusing it. God has blessed you with a wonderfully made mind; in it are indescribable wonders in its ability to operate. He will deliver you in time if you are simply diligent in doing, through faith and by grace, all that He prescribes.

## Answers for Lesson 1

1.  Choices and free will.

2.  Denial, definitions of terms, the anniversary periods, dreams, and the six R's of recovery

3.  Denial

4.  Social, health, finances, legal, and spiritual

7.  Your will, imagination, and curiosity

8.  Sexual immorality

9.  Recognize, realize, repent, receive, rest, and restitution

## Answers for Lesson 2

1.  To allow you the time and fellowship in the Word of God and to have the Holy Spirit do His divine work within you while you read and study. These principles will begin to work on your denial and begin to allow the process of humbling and breaking to take place.

3.  The flesh or sinful nature.

4.  The conscience is the discerning tool for right and wrong. The work of the conscience is independent and direct.

5.  John 14:6

6.  See Romans 8:5-8; 1 Corinthians 2:14; John 6:63.

7.  The evidence of your surrender is the manifested willingness to go to the LORD. You don't turn to other things this time, you turn to Him. The life of Jesus was a life of attraction—not promotion. The benefits He showers you with after your surrender are nothing short of phenomenal. He tells you His way of life is not a burden to follow or imitate and you will find rest for your soul. God tells you that you are free to plan your way, but your answers are from Him. Until you are delivered from self, all your ways are right in your own eyes, your own understanding. The LORD has to weigh your spirit; He has to search you and be allowed to lead and convict you. He is the only one who can make you committed, steadfast, consistent, and sufficient. Only then can you operate in the mind of Christ and your mind is renewed and transformed. After your mind is renewed and transformed, you are then enabled to perform the will of God in your life.

8.  Jesus says belief in Him affects your conscience and actions to the point you are able to entrust Him with your very life. Faith in Him changes your knowledge and understanding of Him. It suddenly helps you to see and understand the things that are unseen and helps you to let go of the things you see and value. You have a change in the perspective of your

reality, values of your treasures, and those things you count as important. Works cause you to boast.

9. The faith God gives you is manifested in such a way you begin to appropriate it in ways that go beyond your logic's ability or strength to understand. It allows you to rest and be still when everything else is going wrong around you. It allows you to know the eye of the lover of your soul and His mighty hand surround you during the time of trial or tribulation. Faith becomes the power that propels you into action. That action becomes the works that others see. The end result is—you are transformed into an overcomer.

10. In John 12:24, you see a mystery about a seed. The flesh cannot bring about the resurrection life you so desperately need. It also shows you the proof of a grace-filled reward that happens in a Christian's life. You have nothing to do with your being born, your life and what it comprises, the work of salvation, or the rewards you will receive in heaven.

## Answers for Lesson 3

1. When you allow God to do the searching, you are secure and at peace. He gives you the desire to start housecleaning. In Principle 4, the process of becoming more of what He wants you to become begins by taking a fearless personal inventory (because of your newfound belief of His unfailing love to you). Read 1 John 3:3.

2. The boundary of liberty is the law and bondage. You can either have a horizontal or a vertical focus.

3. Focus affects six different items in your life: "D" for direction, desires, and devotion, "W" for worship, works, and walk.

4. (1) God hears your requests, (2) your requests are in line with His will, (3) because of your obedience, (4) because of the guidance of the Holy Spirit, you know full well that you have what you ask for.

5. (1) truly believe on the name of His Son, (2) love one another, (3) keep His commandments.

6. 1. to have understanding, be wise, 2. to feel, to think, 2a. to have an opinion of one's self, think of one's self, to be modest, not let one's opinion (though just) of himself exceed the bounds of modesty, 2b. to think or judge what one's opinion is, 2c. to be of the same mind, i.e., agreed together, cherish the same views.

7. Desire, craving, longing, and desire for what is forbidden.

8. To acknowledge. You can begin by asking the Holy Spirit to guide you in identifying to what extent the strengths and weaknesses in your life manifest themselves. It also shows the full extent and truth of your repentance as you do everything possible to have your life restored by Christ.

## Answers for Lesson 4

1.  Because God has given you everything you need to receive and rest in His provisions. In Him alone are you made complete.

2.  A deceptive or misleading method of reasoning.

3.  Sin is defined in three ways. Transgressions, which mean sins you knowingly commit. It means rebellion, sin, trespass. Iniquity means 1. to commit sin without knowledge, to commit sin intrinsically, perversity, depravity, to bend, twist, distort, to do perversely, to be bent, be bowed down, be twisted, be perverted, 2. to commit iniquity, do wrong, pervert. Sin means miss, miss the way, go wrong, incur guilt, to miss the goal or mark, to miss the path of right and duty, to incur guilt, incur penalty by sin, and to forfeit.

4.  Acknowledge means to know, learn to know (become sensitive to), to perceive and see, find out and discern, to discriminate, distinguish, to know by experience, to recognize, admit, acknowledge, confess, to consider. Confess means to: identify, agree, accept and understand what you have done.

5.  You are not able to discern the true nature or depth of pride or sin. It shuts off your communication with God. The Pharisee only prayed to himself but thought his prayers were reaching God. Pride kills and descends, while humility heals and exalts. One causes damnation, while the other causes exaltation.

6.  You will be rewarded for just believing in the Almighty. You cannot allow your faith to grow stale or stagnant. It is impossible to please Him without faith. So once again you see why you cannot have a god of your own understanding—if you do, then you are not using faith. Faith is the substance of things hoped for, the evidence of things not seen. It isn't something you can come up with on your own, and faith of your own understanding is not pleasing God, but self.

## Answers for Lesson 5

1.  A desire for reconciliation is the natural result of the fruit of forgiveness.

2.  You must keep in mind there will be times when you will be prevented from making clean and clear reconciliation. These are times you must be open to the LORD to do His wonderful work of healing and remain willing to be obedient at a moment's notice. These are the times when your faith will be seen as trust. There will also be times reconciliation will not take place but that is not ours to judge. The timing upon which this process takes place and the length of the season with which it takes to complete it is totally up to God. Your heart, in the meantime, must remain open to the possibilities of reconciliation, as well as the possibility of not being able to reconcile, and you must continue to pray for the individual and their healing. When there is a lack of forgiveness and reconciliation, it leaves a vacuum that could be replaced or filled with fear, anger, and the desire to isolate and reject the individual who refuses to reconcile with you. You must be willing to forgive an individual who refuses to forgive and reconcile with you, no matter how much you desire it. You cannot demand forgiveness anymore than you can demand

reconciliation. Remember it is asking for, not demanding of. The actions and results of these two powerful gifts are a result of grace and time.

3. It means one who despises wisdom, who mocks when guilty, who is quarrelsome, and who is licentious.

4. It is being lawless or immoral; it is going beyond customary or proper bounds or limits. It is disregarding rules.

5. It means to be inflated, talk arrogantly, scoff, act as a scorner, and to deride.

6. Sin means to offend, be guilty, trespass, to do wrong, commit an offense, do injury, to be or become guilty, to be held guilty, to be incriminated, to suffer punishment, to declare guilty, to be desolate, and to acknowledge offense.

7. Arrogance is defined in the scriptures in Revelation 3:17. This truth is also spelled out in 1 Corinthians 8:1-2, 10:12.

8. Love is always in the light; hate is a work of darkness.

9. Principle 8 helps you develop a balance between reconciliation and restitution. It prepares your heart and mind to accept the fact this action needs to take place out of obedience, not feeling. It begins to help you practice a willingness to yield to the mighty hand of God. It prepares your heart to put your trust in Him and to believe He does want the best for you and all those in your life. This principle will take time to develop, and the works done in faith will have the most powerful effect of all the things you'll do. It will not only show you the power of grace in your life, but it will show others also. Others will see the work of God in a way they would never have believed, and they will know there is a God when He continues to change you in a consistent manner. The change will be so profound there will be no other explanation for the success.

10. This scripture states you need to keep God's perspective in all you do. You can do this because of the indwelling of the Holy Spirit within you. As you continue to pray, keep your heart open to His influence and guidance, and continue to work with those whom He has sovereignly placed within your life, you can be assured you will accomplish His will with the least amount of pain and suffering in the lives of others, as well as your own.

11. You must remember God knows the heart of both you and the offended. If you have done all that is possible, if you have done all He has laid on your heart to do, if you have sacrificed your will in these matters and had Him conform your will to His, you will have your forgiveness.

12. It will result, first, in persecution because of the contrast in direction and second, in conviction of the hearts surrounding you because they will be affected by their consciences and will hate the light fearing their exposure.

## Answers for Lesson 6

1. It means to count, compute, calculate; to reckon inward, weigh the reasons, to deliberate; meditate on; to suppose, deem, judge; to determine This word deals with reality. This word refers to facts, not suppositions.

2. 1) God's perspective when it comes to your sin, 2) Your hope because of the promises of forgiveness and redemption, 3) God's directions for your God-given change, 4) Your daily practice.

3. When the season of time arrives that you begin to practice applying this principle to your life, you will have already established the habit of obeying and listening to the Holy Spirit and applying what you have read and learned in the Word of God. This obedience was refined through reading and application of the truth of God's Word to your life on a daily basis. It also tells you it is enabled and empowered by the Spirit through the love of others, not through the love of self.

4. The result of new birth is an incorruptible life sealed in God, not in yourself, and yields to the Word of God, which is alive and active. It also abides forever and is thought of as being more valuable than gold, as well as being revered higher than God's name.

5. God and His grace are the only things that will continue to cause you to hunger and thirst for His righteousness.

6. Lying means false or fake. It is untruthfulness, deception, misrepresentation, and/or exaggeration. A lie does three things. 1) It misrepresents the truth. 2) Lying deceives a person. 3) Lying builds a wrong or false relationship, a faulty foundation, a relationship built upon sinking sand. Lying erodes and eventually destroys trust, confidence, love, assurance, security, hope, and lastly, faith.

9. It keeps you operating in the realm of truthfulness. It makes you exercise your conscience on a daily basis.

10. Romans 12:9-21

11. Galatians 5:22-23

12. 1 Corinthians 13:4-8a

13. The vice of love squeezes you and it produces more grace from within you.

14. It means a calling near, exhortation, admonition, encouragement, solace, that which affords comfort or refreshment.

15. It means a persuasive address. Remember, the love of Christ constrains or compels you.

16. "Koinonia," means fellowship, association, community, communion, joint participation.

17. Affection means seat of the tender affections, kindness, benevolence, and compassion; hence your heart. Mercy means emotions, longings, and the manifestations of pity. Pity means to see a need and to supersede the limit of the needed thing; to give more than is needed in order to meet it.

18. It means vain glory, groundless, self-esteem, empty pride, a vain opinion, or error.

19. It means having a humble opinion of one's self, a deep sense of one's (moral) littleness, modesty, humility, and lowliness of mind.

20. It means to lead and to go before.

21. It causes growth and security in both your walk with the Lord, as well as with others.

22. Deceiving is to reckon wrong, to miscount, to cheat by false reckoning, to deceive by false reasoning, to deceive, delude, and to circumvent.

## Answers for Lesson 7

1. You are told to give attention to God's Word. You are to pay attention, become sensitive to, and learn to respond in obedience to its directives. You are also given the word picture of leaning into, to try to listen harder, and by paying closer attention to, through the word incline. You are to focus on God's Word continually and never allow it to depart from your sight. It means the eyes of your heart are to be before the Word to steer you from sin.

2. One of the most pleasing things God loves His children to say back to Him—is His Word.

3. From the Holy Spirit, not from within you or from what you do. In your inner man, not in your muscles. It needs to be of the heart, not of the brain. It needs to be in Him, not of you.

4. Your prayers should not be like the hypocrites and should not cause all the attention to be brought upon the person praying. This is all done for the praise of men, not the praise of God. These men are more mindful of men than of God. Jesus states if there are only men to hear you and if that is who is important to you, then that is all the reward you will get. The praise of men doesn't last long, and it isn't very satisfying or fulfilling.

5. God sees where no man can see and that is in the inner rooms of the heart. He tells you that you should not worry about your rewards or your praise. God is a faithful rewarder. He is just and He never forgets the wages earned, whether it be for good or evil. He states your reward will be seen in the open and revealed to all who are present with Him, that is—all the saints.

6. 1) attitudes, 2) order, 3) a correct focus, 4) adoration

7. The focus of the Apostles' Prayer is on God and others, not so much on you.

9.  The only voice God can and will hear is that of a broken and contrite heart and one who is contrite and poor in spirit. One must be humble in heart, if not he will be resisted by God because of his pride.

10. 1) He is the God of love, 2) He is God, your Father, who created you, 3) He is your Father by covenant because of Jesus, His Son, 4) He grants you His divine nature to operate in this world.

11. You ask Him to lovingly enable you to perform His will, not your own. You ask Him to perform His will through you the same way it is done in the kingdom in heaven, and you acknowledge His will is better than your own.

12. Prayer is the wrestling arena where you exercise, bruise, and bring into submission your will. Your will is the most stubborn and rebellious of all the components of your being.

13. Grace teaches you not to sin. You cannot ask for forgiveness from God unless you truly desire to abstain from sin. Forgiveness is not a turnstile. You cannot continue in your sin as though you were just going in circles. In order to receive forgiveness you must repent. Grace enables you to come to your senses. You truly begin to understand your freedom in Christ. Because of this revelation, you begin to be repulsed by the practice of the sins in your life. You begin to mourn over them and the consequences that transpire in the lives of others, as well as your own. You ask for the guilt and shame caused by the sin to be removed from you. It is here you ask for His holy power to be working in you and the ability to walk in that deliverance.

14. The first and primary meaning of the word tempt is to make trial of a person in order to find out what is truly in him, what he is made of, and what he will do. It points out your true focus. The word tested means to test, try, prove, tempt, assay, put to the proof or test.

15. Sometimes God allows Satan to chasten you in order to change your course or direction. God allows this to happen in order to drive you back to Him or to Him for the first time, to humble you, and to glorify Himself by manifesting more fully to you His ability to preserve you by His power, mercy, and grace.

16. First, He tries you or tests you in order to reveal to you your weakness and your deep need of His grace. Second, He allows the testing because of your need to recognize your need of Him. Third, God allows you to be tested in order to teach you your need to be watchful and prayerful. Fourth, God allows you to be tested in order to cure laziness. Lastly, God allows you to be tested to show you the importance of the armor of God and that your enemies are never flesh and blood, but are the rulers of this world.

17. You have a responsibility to avoid the people, places, and things that would lead you back to these temptations. You must steadfastly resist the devil. You submissively and willingly go to God for grace for the ability to resist familiarity and the devil.

18. They are a providing grace illustrated by the phrase "give us," a pardoning grace illustrated by the phrase "forgive us," a preventing grace illustrated by the phrase "lead us," and lastly, a preserving grace illustrated by the phrase "deliver us."

19. It shows you God alone deserves the credit and praise. It shows you the importance of giving God praise, thanks, and adoration. You are to bring all things to God, and you are to be humble and give Him praise and adoration for His everlasting mercy.

## Answers for Lesson 8

1. Four items manifest that verify the supernatural change that has taken place within your heart and character. These are (1) the ability to humble yourself before God, (2) the desire to be fully dependent upon Him, (3) the ability to accept help from others, and finally, (4) the ability to deny yourself and be a servant to others.

2. When you serve others, you allow the supernatural circulatory system to work. The more you give to others, the more you receive from Him. The more you receive from Him, the more you desire to give in His name. The more grace is revealed and acknowledged from the heart, the more outpouring of gratitude will flow from it. The more gratitude you have, the more you will desire and be enabled to give. The more you give, the more maturity in Christ is manifested and observed and the more you will receive from God to give to others. The more you are changed into the image of Christ, the more you will be aware of your sins. The more you are made aware of your sins, the less you will be apt to lean upon yourself. The less you lean upon yourself, the more humble you will become. The more humble you are made to be, the more God will lift you up. Scripture makes it very clear the longer you abide in Christ, the more the desire will grow within you to be made like Him. This is the direct result of the manifestation of grace within your life.

3. The order of your new priority list in Christ reads like this—Jesus first, others second, and self last. This is a change only God can reveal and manifest within you, and it takes Him to change your narcissistic ways. Only by being a Spirit-filled child of God are you enabled to overcome your self-centeredness and the action it causes which is selfishness. This is a daily battle for the Christian, new or old, and it lasts for a lifetime.

4. It causes an ongoing, one-day-at-a-time, way of living in which you will continue to grow in the Lord and be renewed and transformed daily from faith to faith and glory to glory.

6. Comfort means consolation, a calling near, and summons.

7. Tribulation means a pressing, pressing together, pressure; metaphorically it means oppression, affliction, distress, or straits.

8. It means *to mend (what has been broken or rent), to repair, to complete.* Ethically: *to strengthen, perfect, complete, make one what he ought to be*

9. It means *gentleness, mildness.*

10. Consider your own weakness and susceptibility to temptation before you deal severely with the erring brother, and then restore him in view of that fact.

11. On the positive side, tempted means *to try, make trial of, test: for the purpose of ascertaining his quantity, or what he thinks, or how he will behave himself.* On the negative side it means *to test one maliciously, craftily to put to the proof his feelings or judgments.*

12. The tendency of placing yourself on a higher level than those with whom you are working.

13. One is your weakness and inability to save yourself because you are without strength. The second weakness is man's inability to find his own way to God.

14. You are free to live for yourself and to do what you want but the change that has developed within you causes you to desire to serve your fellow man.

15. You are to be watchful in your prayers, this means you are to lean upon God for all things and allow Him to guide and instruct you.

## Answers for Lesson 9

1. It is not to place you in fear of it happening to you, but to show you it is not something to be afraid of or unavoidable.

2. It is an incident that can be avoided through the daily practice of Godly living, through regular Bible reading, prayer, accountability, fellowship, and serving first in the community of believers and secondly, serving the outside community.

3. The cares of this world, the deceitfulness of riches, the desire for other things, the cares for your family.

4. The Bible declares all decisions are settled in the heart.

5. You are by nature a sinner. You didn't have to be taught or trained to sin; sin is habitual for you. You are trained to react and respond with the world's reactions. As a sinner, it was molded at birth; you are patterned after the first sinners—Adam and Eve.

6. No. Relapse does not begin with the action of again using drugs or alcohol after you have been drug or alcohol-free. It begins in the heart and then affects the mind—in the way you think and make decisions. Your heart and mind have been flawed from the beginning, and you are powerless to change them.

7. Sanctification (to be set apart, and made holy and separate from sin, to grow in the grace of God) enables you to serve the Lord. Jesus completed the work of sanctification when He died for you on the cross. However, the process of sanctification is completed through your love of God, which is demonstrated by your daily obedience to Him through faith. Sanctification establishes your heart through the work of grace. It is a daily process in a Christian's walk.

8. Relapse or backsliding is not a one-time event or set of circumstances. It occurs as a slow and deliberate process of deterioration. It erodes your foundation of sobriety and holy living. There

are several causes of relapse/backsliding. These are your wrong priorities, your half-hearted efforts, and your double-mindedness.

9. Reality is not defined from your perspective. It is not how you think God sees you or what He thinks about you. God's knowledge and love for you define reality. He knows you completely—from beginning to end.

10. Characteristics are defined as your present day habits or practices.

13. The solution is to stay accountable on a daily basis to people who love you. You need to discover the triggers that cause the temptation to run. This habit is usually traceable to unsuccessful attempts at sobriety in the past. And, of course, you need to be obedient to the Word of God.

14. Forsake your old alliances, old friendships, and old behaviors, God will not override your will or choices. These alliances will grow like weeds and soon take over all the good seed you have planted. God reminds the children of Israel He is trustworthy, truthful, and faithful. He will be faithful to bless them but He is also faithful to allow the negative consequences of their choices.

15. Pride

16. You begin to listen to whatever makes you feel good, whether that be ungodly counsel, the world's philosophy, or your own heart. You turn to a sensory or sensual type of faith rather than a foundational, scriptural-based faith. You turn back to old alliances, old patterns, and the rut from which you were delivered. You lie to yourself and to others to cover your sin, and your rut soon turns to a grave. All of your resources are used up, depleted, or carried away.

17. Relationships can alter your focus. If not put into proper perspective, they can cause rapid destruction in your life. If you are not rooted and grounded in Christ, your sobriety can be quickly undone. Your emotions represent one of the most vulnerable areas in building a foundation of sobriety. They have been sheltered and inhibited from the moment you began using in a habitual manner. While you work on building a foundation of sobriety, your emotions beg to be set free and to experience life at its fullest. However, since they've been inhibited for so long, your emotions are immature. Therefore, your emotions need strict governing, guidance, and accountability. The most effective tool the devil uses to attack your emotions is through your sexuality.

18. Your body becomes the temple or tabernacle of God. Satan uses your sexuality to tempt you into sexual sin, which causes you to blaspheme the temple of God. Sexual sin is the only sin you commit against your body.

19. Because you are the tabernacle for the Holy Spirit to dwell in, and it serves Satan well when he brings blaspheming and railing accusations when he accuses you before your Father in heaven on account of your sinful behaviors, words, and deeds. He also incites within you the desire to rebel against the ownership of God who purchased your spirit, soul, and body through the sacrifice of Jesus on the cross.

20. The area of is located just outside your core. Satan knows your need to relate and be needed. Through this area, he can gain an almost unbreakable control of your will and nature. Satan can build a wall of separation between you and God's sovereign purpose to save you because of the strong grip pleasure plays in your being. The secondary response that plays a powerful part in all of this is the area of emotions. Pleasure causes the drive behind the sinful behavior, and the emotions cause the reasoning behind the justification of the sinful behavior. These two powerful sophistries seem to originate from your heart, which at the time appear tried and true. During trials and tribulations of relapse, they try to take control. By combining both (emotions and pleasure), the devil has a potent combination to bring forth condemnation, guilt, and shame. He then uses these as barriers to keep you from believing in a loving, merciful, and forgiving God. God will wash away all of your sins at a moment's notice, if you will just repent, turn, and ask Him to forgive you.

21. It means to be one, to leave a lasting image and impression, to implant firmly on the mind. In the psychological arena it means a learning mechanism operating very early in the life of an animal, in which a particular stimulus immediately establishes an irreversible behavior pattern with references to the same stimulus in the future.

## Answers for Lesson 10

1. It comes through daily reading of God's Word and knowing His unfailing love for you.

2. His wonderful work of sanctification (which means growing in His grace).

3. The main factor which causes all relapse or backsliding is pride.

5. You quit pursuing purity; you become skewed, convoluted, and confused. You lose your potency and become diluted in your walk.

6. Your own wickedness corrects you. This takes the blame game away. You are responsible for your own actions and cannot be the victim when it comes to your sin. You can't blame God or anyone else for getting busted.

7. Because of their poor choices, God allows them to forage in open and unprotected lands. They are vulnerable prey for any predator. He allows Ephraim to keep his choices: his idols and his drink. They commit spiritual adultery, and their authorities love dishonor more than honor.

8. The key to victory over relapse is understanding the difference between self-effort versus being filled with the Spirit and then applying what you know. You try to accomplish things in your own strength and find yourself lacking in strength, resources, and desire. You struggle in the flesh and resist in the spirit. In the carnal mind-set, you cannot operate with the mind of Christ. You are set upon your own resources, focus, and will, and you're settled upon what you are capable of accomplishing or can control. When you are in the flesh or depending upon yourself, you can count on three F's: fatigue, frustration, and failure. On the other hand, when you are filled with the Spirit, you find yourself willing to put forth what seems to be supernatural effort to achieve or accomplish that which you set your mind upon. You are surrendered or resigned to the Lord's will and His leading. When you desire something

and are filled with the Spirit, you surrender your will to the Lord to obtain it. You are more willing to ask for and accept prayer. You have an open mind-set and desire for accountability. You are teachable, humble, and broken in accepting whatever God desires to give you.

9. Confession is admitting with your mouth and agreeing with God you have done wrong.

10. Repentance means turning away from sin and turning toward God.

11. Restoration means being put back into right standing with God.

12. You begin the process of renewing your mind. You accomplish this by daily washing your mind with the scriptures and the Holy Spirit.

13. The Word of God and the Holy Spirit perform the work within you. Only God, through the use of His Word, can accomplish this miraculous work. The Word has the power to divide the spirit from the soul so you can worship God in spirit and truth. It also allows you to understand what the Spirit says to you. Your mind needs to be washed and renewed through the Holy Spirit. God doesn't ask you to do anything unreasonable. He has already done everything for you and simply asks you to follow in His steps.

14. You need God's help to offer things that are acceptable to Him. You need God's mercies in order to present yourself as a living sacrifice because you must be holy and acceptable to God. Only through the blood of Jesus can you be made clean and pure.